Patterns and Projects
for the Scroll Saw

PATTERNS
and
PROJECTS
for the
SCROLL SAW

Joyce C. Nelson
and
John A. Nelson

Stackpole Books

Published by
STACKPOLE BOOKS
Cameron and Kelker Streets
P.O. Box 1831
Harrisburg, PA 17105

Printed in the United States of America

First Edition

10 9 8 7 6 5 4 3 2 1

Library of Congress Cataloging-in-Publication Data
Nelson, John A., 1935–
    Patterns and projects for the scroll saw / John A. Nelson and
Joyce C. Nelson. — 1st ed.
        p.   cm.
    ISBN 0-8117-3040-9
    1. Jig saws. 2. Woodwork. I. Nelson, Joyce C. II. Title.
TT186.N44   1991
684′.083—dc20
                                                        90-44284

CONTENTS

INTRODUCTION

The ever-increasing popularity of the constant-tension scroll saw comes as no surprise to anyone who has used this versatile power tool. It can produce the extremely tight internal and external curves necessary for intricate designs and small projects. With a variable speed control, wood, plastic, metal, and—with a diamond blade—even glass can be cut. Yet it is so easy to use and produces such a smooth cut that most anyone can achieve professional results with a scroll saw in a very short time.

Woodworking with a scroll saw is a great way to relax and at the same time be creative. You can use your scroll saw to turn scrap wood into useful projects, from toys to practical household items to beautiful gifts. Whether you keep your projects for yourself, give them as gifts, or sell them at crafts fairs and bazaars, the satisfaction you get from your own labor will stay with you.

Do you already have a scroll saw? If so, these patterns and projects will provide you with hours of woodworking fun. If not, the first chapter of this book is designed to get you started. It points out the major features to consider when purchasing a saw, provides general information on many currently available models, discusses blade selection, and outlines the basics of scroll saw use.

You will find over 340 patterns in this book. There are a large number of simple patterns, as well as eight styles of alphabets and numerals. Several two- and three-piece projects and about ten advanced, multipiece projects are included. A scroll saw is the only tool necessary to make most of the projects in this book. A few projects may require a drill, a handsaw, or a hammer.

Very fine details are easily reproduced with a scroll saw. (Photo courtesy of Advanced Machinery Imports, Ltd.)

Scroll saw projects are fun and easy to make—and beautiful as well. (Photo courtesy of Advanced Machinery Imports, Ltd.)

Do not feel restricted to using the patterns exactly as illustrated. Enlarge them, reduce them, change them for your own needs. Any pattern can be used many ways: a wall clock pattern, with very little modification, can be used to make a puzzle, a door stop, or a pull toy. Your imagination will help you come up with new ways to use these patterns.

We hope you will enjoy many hours of pleasure making these patterns and projects. If you have any suggestions or comments about this book, we would love to hear from you.

Joyce C. Nelson and John A. Nelson
Peterborough, New Hampshire

The Scroll Saw

If you do not already own a scroll saw, there are several things you should consider before you make your purchase. To realize the most pleasure from scroll sawing, you will want to get the best possible saw for the amount you can spend. And to do that, you need to know what you want. Different saws have different features; the following information will help you determine what to look for as you begin to shop for your own scroll saw.

SAW ANATOMY

Since colonial times woodworkers have wanted a tool that could cut intricate designs. The earliest scroll saws were handmade of wood and they had crude metal blades. Around 1850 or so, metal scroll saws began to appear in America. They were footpowered by treadle or pedal mechanisms. By the turn of the century, electric motors were added to the scroll saw.

The conventional scroll saw had a blade driven by an arm at one end and a spring at the other. The problem with these older models was that the blade tension wasn't constant. The new scroll saws eliminate this problem. The blade on a constant-tension saw is attached at both ends to rigid, parallel arms. It moves slightly backward on the upstroke and slightly forward on the downstroke, achieving a beautifully smooth cut every time. The new machines are also lighter, they create very little dust, and they are the quietest of all stationary power tools.

Today's scroll saws have either *fixed speed* or *variable speed* motors. Fixed speed saws operate at only one speed. That speed depends on the saw you buy; the range is 1,200 to 3,450 cutting strokes per minute (csm). Variable speed saws can be adjusted from full stop to the saw's maximum, usually about 2,000 csm. Most scroll saw motors are rated in either amperes or horsepower. They range from 0.9 A to 3.6 A and from $1/20$ Hp to $1/4$ Hp. The higher the amperage, the more powerful the motor. Underpowered saws will not hold up with moderate to heavy use, so it's best to get a motor with as much power as you can.

The *throat depth* is the maximum width you can put through the scroll saw and is a function of the length of the arm. This measurement varies from model to model, usually between 14 and 24 inches. Saws with very large throat depth tend to have more vibration than smaller ones. A good choice for the average woodworker is a saw with an 18-inch throat.

Most scroll saws have a 2-inch *cutting capacity*, the distance between the blade mount and the table. This means the thickest piece of wood you can cut is 2 inches thick.

The way in which the blade is attached to the arm is one of the features that vary considerably from saw to saw. Manufacturers are always coming up with new designs for *blade mounts*; they know the consumer

The variable-speed control is an optional feature that allows you to easily adjust the cutting speed of the blade. (Photo courtesy of Advanced Machinery Imports, Ltd.)

Throat depth is measured from the blade to the inside of the back support for the arm. This saw has a throat depth of 14³/₈ inches. (Photo courtesy of Advanced Machinery Imports, Ltd.)

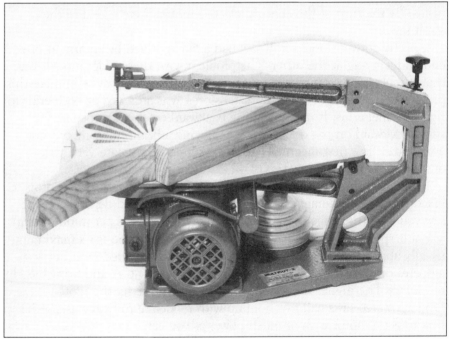

wants to be able to change blades quickly and easily without sacrificing the safety of a well-secured blade. Before you buy a particular saw, try changing the blade. If the procedure is complicated and awkward, it will inevitably interfere with the usefulness of the saw.

The sizes and shapes of worktables vary considerably. Larger tables tend to be more useful. The surface of the table should be unflawed with a smooth finish. Some tables have a tilt feature, which occasionally comes in handy. A tilt of 15 to 20 degrees in one direction is adequate.

Many saws have a *dust blower* option. As you make a cut, the sawdust produced can cover your pattern lines. The dust blower keeps it out of your way.

The adjustable *hold-down* is simply a guide that holds the work against the tabletop while you are making a cut. As you get more experience using the saw, you may find the hold-down gets in your way and use it less often.

One accessory we recommend highly is the *foot switch*. The foot switch allows you to have both hands on the workpiece at all times; you won't have to take one hand off the work to turn the saw on or off. This is not merely a convenience; it is also an important safety consideration.

Scroll saws range in price from just under $100 to $2,000 or so. The more you intend to use your saw, the more you should be prepared to spend. Higher-quality saws cost more, but they are better able to withstand heavy use, and they frequently outperform cheaper models. The rule of thumb—for scroll saws as well as other tools—is always purchase the best tool you can afford at the time. The better tool usually does a better job and is often safer and easier to use. We recommend against any saw under $200; most scroll saws in this price range lack a rigid parallel-arm design and do not have adequate safety and performance features.

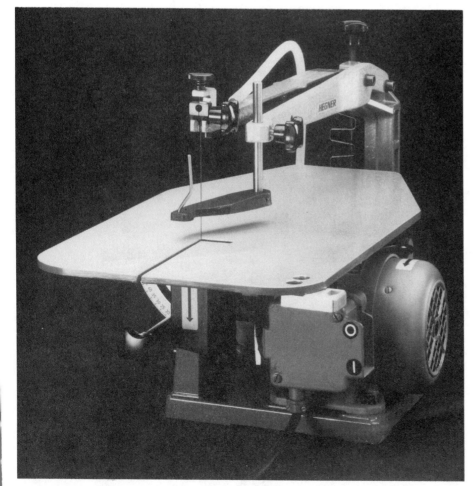

The hold-down is like an extra hand, which can hold your workpiece flat against the tabletop while you operate the saw. (Photo courtesy of Advanced Machinery Imports, Ltd.)

WHAT'S AVAILABLE

There are several models of scroll saws on the market today. They come with a wide variety of features and in a broad range of prices. Your scroll saw is a major purchase, and doing some homework before you buy is a good way to make sure you get what you want at a price you can afford. A few saws are discussed below to give you a feel for what's available.

An inexpensive parallel-arm scroll saw with many of the same features as more expensive saws is sold by **American Machine and Tool**. It has a solid, heavy-duty cast-iron base and table. Model 4601 features a dust blower.

General specifications for the AMT-4601: $^1/_8$ Hp, fixed-speed motor, $15^3/_4$-inch throat depth, 2-inch cutting capacity, $7^7/_8$- by $14^3/_4$-inch tabletop that tilts up to 45 degrees.

For years **Delta** manufactured a fixed-arm scroll saw that was top-of-the-line. I've had mine since 1971. Although the fixed-arm scroll saws still have a place in some woodshops, the newer scroll saw designs of today can do much more. Delta's most recent models have a C-arm design. In place of the two parallel arms found on most saws, Delta uses a single horseshoe-shaped arm. Their new 18-inch model features a variable-speed motor with a digital speed readout. The circular table tilts 30 degrees to the left and 45 degrees to the right, and can rotate 90 degrees to tilt 15 degrees up and 30 degrees down.

General specifications for the Delta-18: variable-speed motor with cutting speeds of 40 to 2,000 csm, 18-inch throat depth, 2-inch cutting capacity, 16-inch diameter tilting tabletop.

Dremel has been known for many years for their excellent line of

The AMT-4601, manufactured by American Machine and Tool.

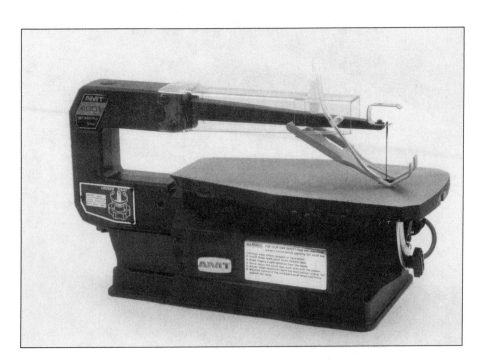

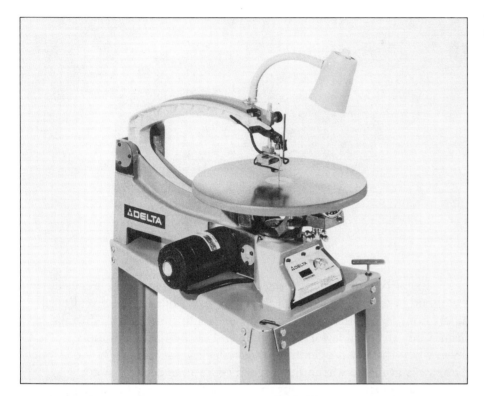

The Delta-18. (Photo courtesy of Delta International Machinery Corp.)

The Dremel-1671. (Photo courtesy of Dremel.)

small woodworking tools. They have added a full-size scroll saw, model 1671, to their line. It has two features we especially like. The built-in blade storage case is handy, and the built-in blade length gauge gives an accurate measurement of the exact distance between blade holders.

General specifications for the Dremel-1671: two-speed motor, low speed (890 csm) is $1/20$ Hp and high speed (1,790 csm) is $1/10$ Hp, 16-inch throat depth, 2-inch cutting capacity, 12-inch diameter tabletop with up to 45-degree tilt.

The Excalibur II. (Photo courtesy of Excalibur Machine and Tool Co.)

Excalibur has two nice scroll saws on the market: the heavy-duty Excalibur 24 and, for home hobbyists, the Excalibur II. The Excalibur II differs from many other saws in the blade holding and driving mechanism. Only the final few inches at the end of the blade arm move up and down when the saw is operating, thus reducing the amount of vibration. The saw is available with a three-speed or a variable-speed motor.

General specifications for the Excalibur II: $1/4$ Hp, variable-speed motor (6 to 1,800 csm) or $1/4$ Hp motor with three-step pulleys (400, 800, and 1,400 csm), 19-inch throat depth, $1^3/4$-inch cutting capacity, 12- by $17^1/4$-inch tabletop with up to 45-degree tilt to left and right.

The **Heartwood** scroll saw, manufactured by Glendo Corporation, comes complete with a heavy-gauge steel stand. It features machined aluminum arms and a built-in dust blower. It also has a built-in blade installation fixture.

General specifications for the Heartwood: $1/4$ Hp, two-speed motor, low speed is 1,100 csm and high speed is 1,700 csm, 18-inch throat depth, 2-inch cutting capacity, large tabletop with up to 45-degree tilt to left and right.

Hegner is one of the top-end saws. It is manufactured in West Germany and imported by Advanced Machinery Imports Ltd. The Multimax-2, Multimax-3, Polymax, and the new Multimax-18 are their most popular models. The blade suspension system gives the saw precise cutting ability, and the blades can be easily and quickly changed. All models have built-in dust blowers and hold-down arms.

General specifications for the Multimax-2: 1.9 A, fixed-speed motor (1,660 csm), $14^3/8$-inch throat depth, 2-inch cutting capacity, 9- by 17-inch tabletop with up to 45-degree tilt left.

The **Jet** is another nice, inexpensive scroll saw. It is similar in design to the AMT model and has many of the same features. A three-legged stand is available as an option.

General specifications for the Jet DSS-15 DIY: $1/8$ Hp, fixed-speed motor (1,725 csm), 15-inch throat depth, 2-inch cutting capacity, 8- by $16^1/2$-inch tabletop with up to 45-degree tilt right.

The **R.B.I. Hawk-20** is a top-end scroll saw. R.B. Industries was the first American company to develop and market a full line of scroll

The Heartwood. (Photo courtesy of Glendo Corporation.)

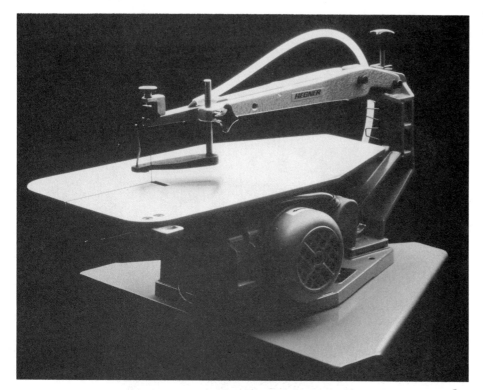

The Hegner Multimax-2. (Photo courtesy of Advanced Machinery Imports, Ltd.)

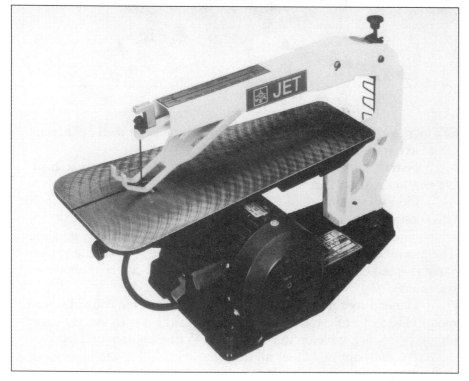

The Jet DSS-15. (Photo courtesy of Jet Equipment and Tools.)

saws. The design of the Hawk-20 incorporates a convenient cam-lock tension adjustment, which gives automatic blade tensioning every time. The saw also features a dust blower.

General specifications for the Hawk-20: $1/8$ Hp, two-speed motor, low speed is 695 csm and high speed is 1,110 csm, 20-inch throat depth,

▲ The R.B.I. Hawk-20. (Photo courtesy of R.B. Industries.)

► The Craftsman-23613. (Photo courtesy of Sears.)

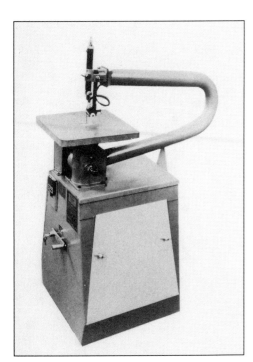

The Vega 126-S1. (Photo courtesy of Vega Enterprises.)

1³/₄-inch cutting capacity, 13³/₄- by 22¹/₂-inch tabletop with 30-degree tilt to left and 45-degree tilt to right.

Sears enters the scroll saw market with a 13-inch saw. It is small but features a heavy cast-iron base and a two-position blade holder.

General specifications for the Craftsman-23613: fixed-speed motor (1,700 csm), 13-inch throat depth, 1-inch cutting capacity.

The **Vega** saw is made with great attention to durability and safety. The machine is mounted on a very heavy enclosed steel base, and the variable-speed control is lockable so that low speeds can be assured for beginners.

General specifications for the Vega 126-S1: ¹/₃ Hp, variable-speed motor (430 to 1,725 csm), 26-inch throat depth, 1¹/₂-inch cutting capacity, 14- by 14-inch tabletop that tilts up to 45 degrees right and left.

An excellent way to see all the latest models is to attend a woodworking show near you. The Woodworking Association of North America sponsors twelve to fifteen shows a year at which most all large companies display their latest tools. Write to the WANA at P.O. Box 706, Plymouth, NH 03264, and ask for information about a woodworking show near you. You might want to join their organization to get their bi-monthly magazine, *International Woodworking*, as well as bonus projects and special discounts from participating companies.

BLADES

There are two major kinds of blades used in today's scroll saws, plain end and pin type. Most saws accept both kinds. Plain-end blades offer a wide variety of sizes and types and produce a superior cut. The pin-type blades are easier to put in and remove from the machine.

Most scroll saws use 5-inch-long blades. The blades are very narrow to facilitate tight turns. They range in size from .012 inch wide and .006 inch thick to 1/4 inch wide and .028 inch thick. Generally, the narrower the blade, the more teeth per inch. The range is about 9 to 28 teeth per inch. Finer blades with a higher number of teeth per inch are available for specialty work, such as cutting brass or aluminum.

Skiptooth blades are also available for scroll saw work. They differ from regular blades in that they have wider spaces in between the teeth. These spaces provide faster, cooler cutting and positive chip clearance. Plastic and fibrous materials tend to clog regular blades, but they are cleared with the skiptooth blade.

Spiral blades increase your saw's versatility and allow you to do things you can't do with a flat blade. With a spiral blade you can handle oversize work that normally wouldn't fit in your saw, cut complex bevels without changing your table set-up, saw extra-wide saw kerf projects with only one cut, and saw intricate patterns without having to turn your workpiece.

The two major kinds of scroll saw blades are pin type (left) and plain end (right).

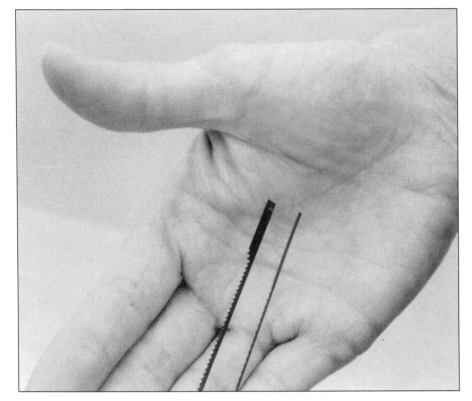

17

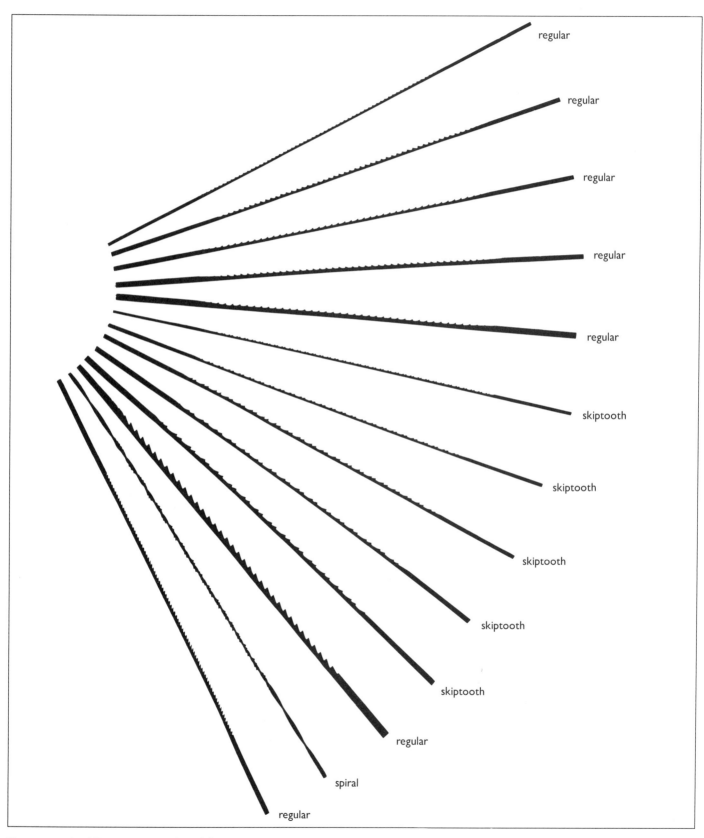

regular

regular

regular

regular

regular

skiptooth

skiptooth

skiptooth

skiptooth

skiptooth

regular

spiral

regular

You can see the differences among these full-size regular, skiptooth, and spiral blades. Notice the range in the number of teeth per inch.

Scroll saw blades are very inexpensive. They range between 25 and 50 cents or so each, depending on the type of blade and the quantity purchased. Poor quality control is one consequence of the low cost. Even identical blades of the same size and tooth count will not always cut the same way or last the same length of time.

Almost any job you do can be performed with a variety of blade sizes. Experiment with several kinds of blades to see what works best for you. Larger, wider blades with fewer teeth per inch will generally cut faster and last longer, but smaller, narrower blades with more teeth per inch will produce finer detail and a smoother edge. Use the largest blade that still gives you satisfactory detail and finish. You'll get good performance while maintaining maximum sawing speed and blade life.

Remember that the thinner the material, the finer the blade. You will have to adjust your rate of feed into the blade depending upon the blade you're using and the thickness of the stock. A 2-inch-thick piece of wood requires a much slower rate of feed than a $1/4$-inch-thick piece would, given the same blade. Be sure to keep at least three full teeth in contact with the material at all times. For example, if you're cutting $1/4$-inch thick wood, you'll need a blade with at least 12 teeth per inch. Never force the wood into the blade; let the blade cut its way through the wood at its own rate.

Here are some basic guidelines for selecting blades:

▪ There is no "right" blade for a particular job. Each size of blade will accommodate a range of thicknesses and materials.

▪ Generally, the finer the blade, the lower the maximum thickness of the material, the smoother the cut, and the slower the rate of feed. And of course, the more blade breakage.

▪ Select the coarsest blade that will give you a cut that is smooth enough for your project.

▪ With practice you will be able to sense which blade can give you the best compromise of smoothness, speed, and durability for the project at hand.

TIPS AND TECHNIQUES

Most scroll saws on the market today are well made and give exceptional performance. Their manufacturers, however, seem to assume that anyone who purchases a scroll saw already knows how to use one. They provide the bare minimum of operating instructions (and perhaps a few patterns), but they don't provide the basics of how to actually start using the scroll saw. In this section, we'll present some general information on how to get your saw up and running.

Since each saw has a slightly different blade attachment mechanism, you'll have to consult your operator's manual to see how to attach the blade to the saw. Most saws come with the blade in place, but the blade has to be tightened before you can use it. Tighten the blade using the blade tension knob, usually located at the top and back of the arm.

Pluck the blade with one hand and turn the knob to tighten the blade. If you have a good sense of pitch, tune it to high C. For those without a musical ear, continue plucking and tightening until the blade gives off a clear, high-pitched tone. Get it tight, but not so tight that the blade breaks. Experiment with the tension knob and remember, the blades are cheap, you can afford to break a few. On saws that use blade clamps you must loosen the top thumb screw to leave a small gap so that the clamp can pivot freely. **Always loosen the blade when you're done for the day. Do not leave the saw blade tight when it's not in use.**

Using the base of a carpenter's square or a small drafter's triangle, check that the saw blade is 90 degrees to the tabletop. If not, adjust the tabletop.

Before you begin cutting, make yourself comfortable at the saw. You should be able to move your workpiece around the tabletop without stretching or straining. For long hours at the saw, sitting may cause less fatigue than standing.

Your scroll saw is very versatile, but perhaps its most exciting feature is its ability to make inside cuts. Using a drill, make a small hole in the center of the area to be cut out. The hole should be just a little larger than the saw blade width. Then release the tension on the scroll saw blade and disconnect the top of the blade from the blade clamp. Insert the end of the blade through the hole in your workpiece, reattach the blade to the blade clamp, and retighten the tension of the blade. You can now make the cut as usual.

If you need two or more exact copies of the same pattern, simply tape several pieces of wood together and cut them all out at once. Remember, the total height of the stack cannot exceed the cutting depth of your saw. Be sure the parts don't slip while you're cutting. You will have to retape the stack as you cut.

A properly tightened blade will emit a clear, high-pitched tone when plucked. Remember to loosen the blade when you're done using the saw.

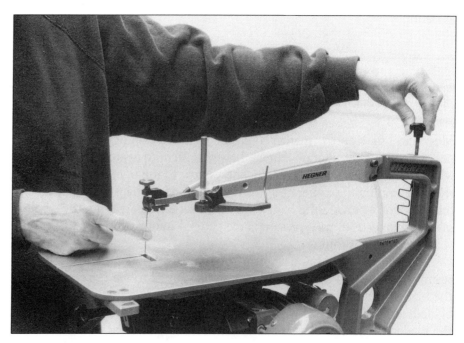

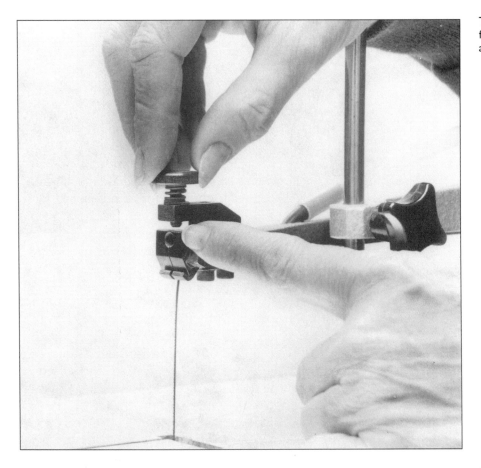

This small gap allows the blade clamp to pivot freely. If your saw has a different kind of blade attachment, you won't have to worry about this.

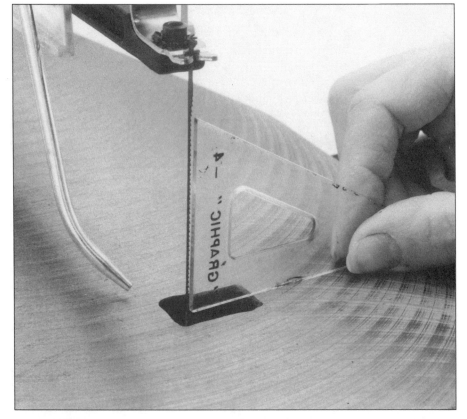

Before you begin to cut, make sure your blade makes a 90-degree angle with the tabletop.

To make an inside cut, drill a small hole, just a little larger than the width of the blade, in the section to be cut out. Then disconnect the top of the blade and slide the workpiece down the blade. Reattach and retighten the blade and you're ready to cut.

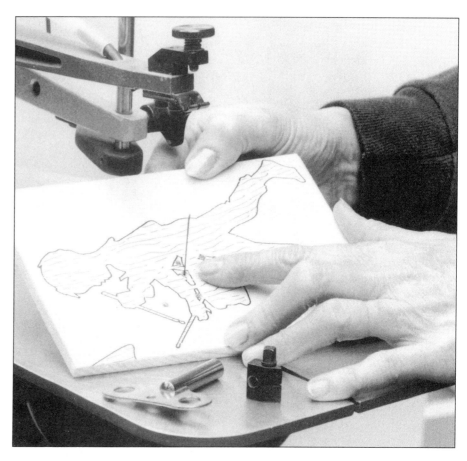

Whenever you need several pieces that are the same size and shape, tape a stack of pieces of wood together and cut them all at once.

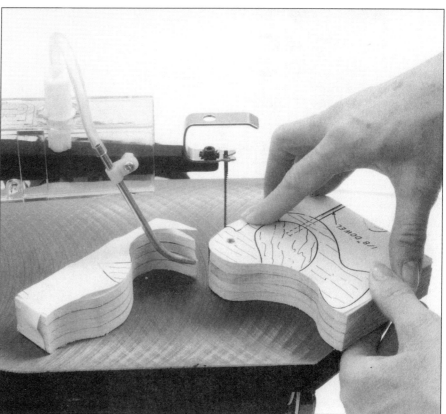

If you have to saw very thin material and you're worried that it may splinter or shatter, tape the material to a piece of corrugated cardboard and cut them out together. Again, remember to retape as you cut out the pattern.

You can easily handle a very small piece by taping it to a larger piece of wood with double-faced masking tape. The larger piece makes it easier to move the pattern around the blade. After the cut is made, separate the two pieces.

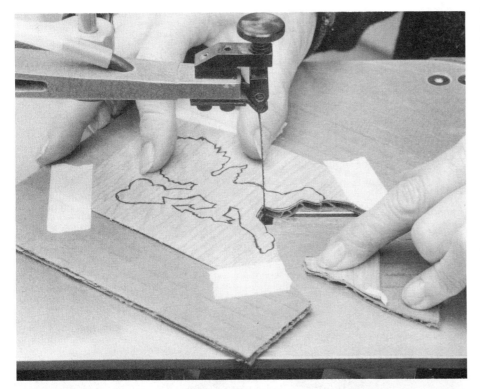

You can cut very thin pieces without fear of splintering them if you tape them to a piece of corrugated cardboard.

It is easier to manipulate a very small piece if you attach it to a larger piece of wood using double-faced masking tape.

The compound cutting technique allows you to use your scroll saw to make fully three-dimensional figures. Cut the pattern out on one surface and retape the cut-out parts back in place so that you can see the lines of the pattern. Make the second cuts on the other surface (90 degrees from the first). Now remove the pieces you taped in place and your project is complete.

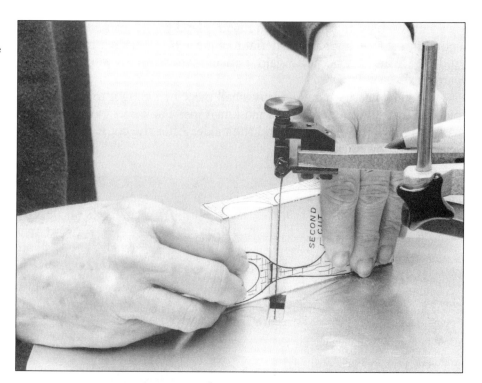

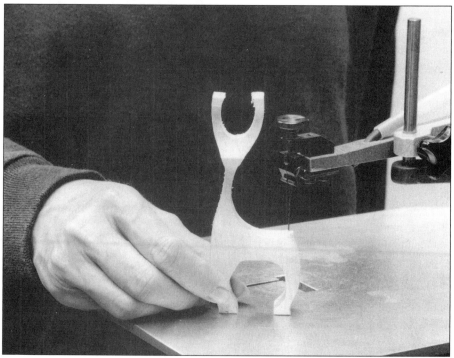

Compound cutting allows you to make interesting projects with cuts in three dimensions. There will be two patterns, one for the first cut and one for the second. Trace the patterns on two adjacent sides of a single block of wood. Cut out the pattern from one surface and then retape the cut-off pieces back in place. Rotate the block 90 degrees and make the second cut.

Selecting Materials and Supplies

With the right blades, your scroll saw will cut several kinds of materials, from wood and plastic to metal. Most of the projects in this book have been made from hardwood, softwood, or plywood, but you can adapt them to other materials.

Hardwood comes from deciduous trees, which shed their leaves each fall, such as maple, oak, and cherry. Hardwood is generally more difficult to saw than softwood, but it is stronger and takes a finish better. Use hardwood for projects like toys, which need to hold up under heavy use.

Softwood comes from evergreens, such as pine, fir, and spruce. Softwood is especially suitable for decorative painted projects.

Plywood is wood made up in layers for strength and uniformity. There are several grades of plywood; use a high grade for satisfactory results with these projects. Plywood in thicknesses of $1/8$ inch, $3/16$ inch, and $1/4$ inch usually has to be ordered by mail. The addresses of suppliers can be found in the appendix.

Wood from your local lumberyard is probably sold by its rough size, that is, before the surface is planed. After planing, a 1-by-6-inch board will actually measure closer to $3/4$ by $5^{1}/_{2}$ inches. Remember this when you're getting specific sizes of wood for these projects. (The suppliers

Many of the items you need to complete your projects can be purchased ready-made from catalogs.

noted in the appendix provide wood that is planed and sanded to the required size.) Always purchase high-quality, knot-free, straight-grained wood. Since you will be using only small quantities of wood for these projects, it won't cost that much more to get a higher-quality wood.

Many of the projects require dowels. Dowels made of birch or maple can be found at any local lumberyard in a wide variety of diameters. If you want dowels of oak, mahogany, or walnut, you will have to order them by mail. Again, see the appendix for suppliers.

Some projects require special parts, such as wheels, pins, axles, and music boxes. The appendix lists many suppliers who specialize in items of this sort. Send for their catalogs; they'll give you even more ideas for woodworking projects.

Enlarging or Reducing a Pattern or Design

All of the simple patterns and most of the multipiece projects in this book can be made in any size. If you wish to enlarge or reduce a pattern, there are four ways you can go about it. The method you use makes no difference in the final outcome of the project.

One of the simplest and least expensive ways to alter the size of a pattern is to use a photocopier. Newer machines include a feature that enlarges or reduces. Simply choose the enlargement or reduction mode and make a copy. For extreme reductions or enlargements, the process might take two or more steps; reduce the reduction (or enlarge the enlargement) until you get the size you want.

Another quick method, one that is extremely accurate, is to get a PMT, or photomechanical transfer, of the design made at a local printing shop. This photographic method can provide exact enlargements or reductions without any effort on your part. Prices will range from $5 to $15, depending on the size of the final PMT. If your time is valuable, this method might be worth the cost.

The pantograph is a drawing tool, whose adjustable arms can enlarge or reduce to most any size. If you do a lot of enlarging or reducing, this tool may be well worth its modest price ($5 to $15).

The method most often used by woodworkers is the "grid and dot-to-dot" method. It is very simple, doesn't require the skills of an artist, and can be used to enlarge or reduce to any size or scale. A few basic drafting tools, including a drafting board, a scale (a simple ruler will do), a T-square, a 45-degree triangle, and masking tape would be helpful, but you can improvise with what you have at home. Follow these seven steps to adapt any pattern to the size you want.

Step 1. Make a copy of the original pattern and draw a grid over it. The size of the original grid often depends on the intricacy of the original pattern. In the example on the next page we've used an original grid of 1/8 inch. For a less detailed pattern we might have selected a larger original grid. Now decide on the size you want for the finished project. We've made the final size twice as large as the original. This means the final grid will have to be twice as big as the original grid, or 1/4 inch.

Step 2. Start from the upper left corner and write the letters of the alphabet from left to right on the original grid. From the same starting point, number the squares to the bottom. In this example, the letters run horizontally along the top from A through R and the numbers go from 1 through 28.

Step 3. Tape a blank sheet of paper to the drafting board and care-

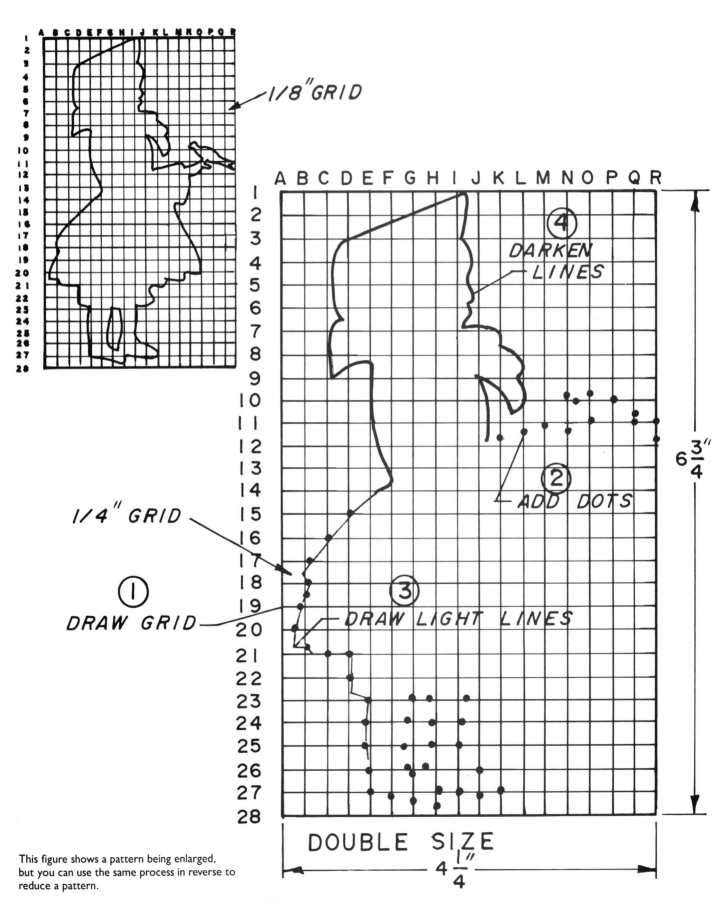

1/8″ GRID

1/4″ GRID

① DRAW GRID

③ DRAW LIGHT LINES

② ADD DOTS

④ DARKEN LINES

DOUBLE SIZE
4 1/4″

6 3/4″

This figure shows a pattern being enlarged, but you can use the same process in reverse to reduce a pattern.

fully draw the required final grid, using the same number of horizontal and vertical lines.

Step 4. On your final grid, mark letters and numbers the same way.

Step 5. On the original, mark dots along the pattern outline wherever it crosses a line.

Step 6. On your final grid, carefully locate and draw dots corresponding to the ones you marked on the original. Be sure to use the numbers and letters to guide you.

Step 7. Connect the dots. You do not have to be exact. Simply sketch lines between the dots.

TRANSFERRING THE PATTERN FROM PAPER TO WOOD

Sand the top and bottom surfaces of your wood until they are very smooth before you transfer the pattern. You will be able to see the pattern much better on a smooth, clean surface and your workpiece will move around the tabletop more easily if there are no snags on the wood.

Before you position your pattern on the wood, note the direction of the grain. Then place your pattern on the wood so that any extended features, such as an animal's legs or tail, are parallel to the grain. Some-

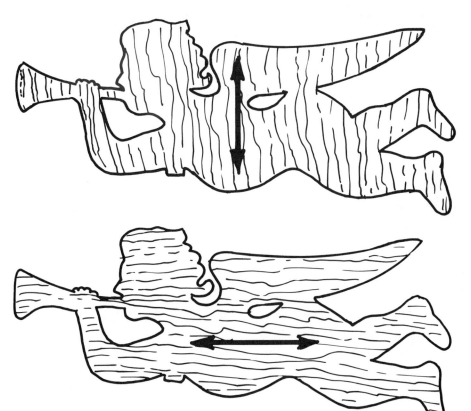

The upper figure shows a poorly placed pattern. With this orientation, small pieces such as the feet, horn, and wing tip can break off easily. The lower figure shows the correct placement of the pattern in relation to the grain of the wood.

Transferring a pattern by using a wood-burning set or a hot iron is easy. Place a photocopy of the pattern facedown on the wood and trace over the pattern outline. Remove the paper and there's your pattern.

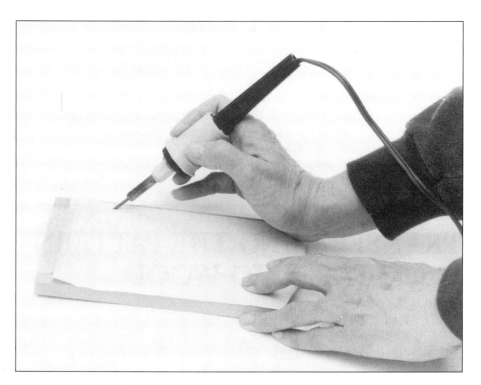

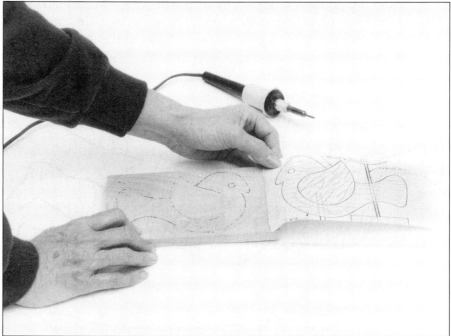

times features go both ways, so you may have to place the pattern diagonal to the wood grain. The thin areas may break off if you don't pay careful attention to the direction of the grain.

There is a very simple, quick, clean method for transferring a pattern (8½ by 11 inches or smaller) to a single piece of wood. First, make a photocopy of the pattern. Then tape the copy, printed side down, to the wood. Using a hot flat iron or wood-burning set, heat the back side of the copy; the pattern will be transferred from the paper directly to the wood.

You can also make a photocopy and, using rubber cement, glue the copy directly to the wood. You will then have a clean, sharp image for the pattern. The paper can be easily removed after you make the cuts.

Another quick method is to place a sheet of carbon paper between the pattern and the wood. Then simply trace the pattern. This method works well for patterns larger than 8½ by 11 inches, but you'll need large sheets of carbon paper. Meisel Hardware Specialties sells 17- by 22-inch sheets of carbon paper (refer to no. 7347 when ordering). One drawback

For intricate patterns, such as this one, you need a clean copy of the pattern. Use rubber cement to attach the pattern directly to the wood and then cut out the pattern. The paper will come off easily after you're finished sawing.

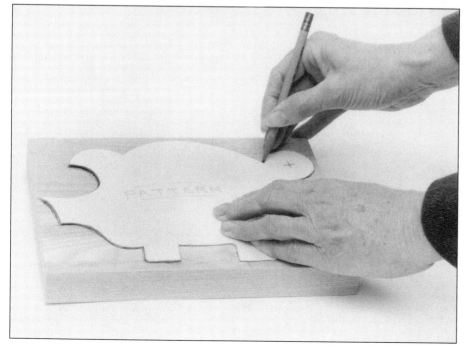

Make a template for patterns you'll use several times.

to this method is that it tends to leave smudges on the wood that can be difficult to remove.

If you intend to make several pieces from the same pattern, transfer the pattern to a sheet of heavy cardboard or 1/8-inch plywood and cut it out. You can then retrace around this template as often as necessary.

If the pattern is symmetrical—the exact same size and shape on both sides of a line that bisects the pattern—make only half a pattern and trace it twice, once on each side of a line you draw on the wood. This will ensure perfect symmetry of the finished project.

Finishing

Accurate blade movement and high cutting speed assure not only effective sawing, but also a superior finish. This is what makes a scroll saw such a time- and energy-efficient tool. The saw blade leaves a beautifully finished edge on all cuts, minimizing or eliminating altogether the need to sand the edges. Sanding is required only on the surfaces.

You will want to finish many of these projects by painting them. Use an oil-based primer as the base coat. For the top coat, oil-based paint works well but requires a long drying time. Latex gloss enamel is a better choice for a quick finish on multicolored projects. It dries fast and you can apply several colors at one work session. Always use nontoxic, nonlead paint for children's toys. For a pattern with intricate details, stencil them or paint them by hand. An ink pen or a woodburning tool can be used for very fine details.

You may prefer a clear natural finish on some of your projects. Deft is a quick-drying, brush-on lacquer that gives you a beautiful natural finish. Give your project three or four thin coats of Deft, sanding lightly between each application. Deft, like many other wood finishes, has a strong, unpleasant odor, so apply your finish in a well-ventilated room.

An antique finish will give your projects extra character. Paint the project as usual, then sand it in spots where it would have worn through the years. Apply a walnut stain to all surfaces and quickly wipe it off. The stain will stay in the abraded surfaces, giving your project an aged look.

Regardless of the kind of finish you use on your projects, two or three light coats will give you better results than one thick coat. Sand lightly between coats, using 0000 steel wool or 220-grit sandpaper. After the final coat of paint or stain has dried, apply a light coat of paste wax. The paste wax will protect your project and give it a satiny look and feel. The final finish is what everyone sees, so take your time and do a good job.

Suede Finish

There are certain projects where you may want the soft look and feel of suede: for padding on the inside of a jewelry box, for a protective bottom surface on magazine or book racks, for a furry texture on an animal project. Suede-Tex is an easy-to-use product that gives you this kind of textured, fabric-like finish. It comes in several colors and can be purchased from DonJer Products in New Jersey. Be sure to order the inexpensive spray gun necessary to apply the fibers and the special thinner you'll need to thin the adhesive and to clean your brush. **Although Suede-Tex makes an attractive finish for many projects, it may be toxic and is unsuitable as a finish for children's toys.**

How to Read the Patterns

All projects in this book are intended to be cut from materials that are 2 inches or less in thickness to accommodate the cutting depth of most saws. If no suggested thickness is given, you may use whatever size suits you.

A number in parentheses following the name of a piece tells you how many of each to cut.

Broken lines indicate hidden surfaces or features of the project. Some projects are shown in an exploded view, which illustrates the project as it is to be put together. Study the drawings until you fully understand how the project is to be assembled.

Patterns and
Projects

37

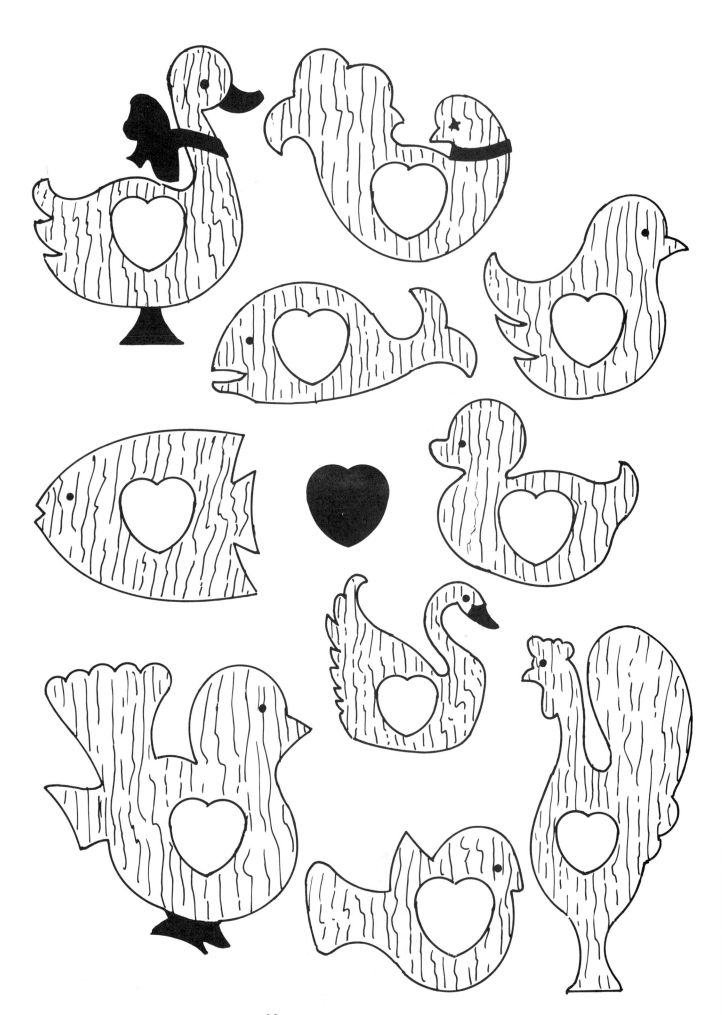

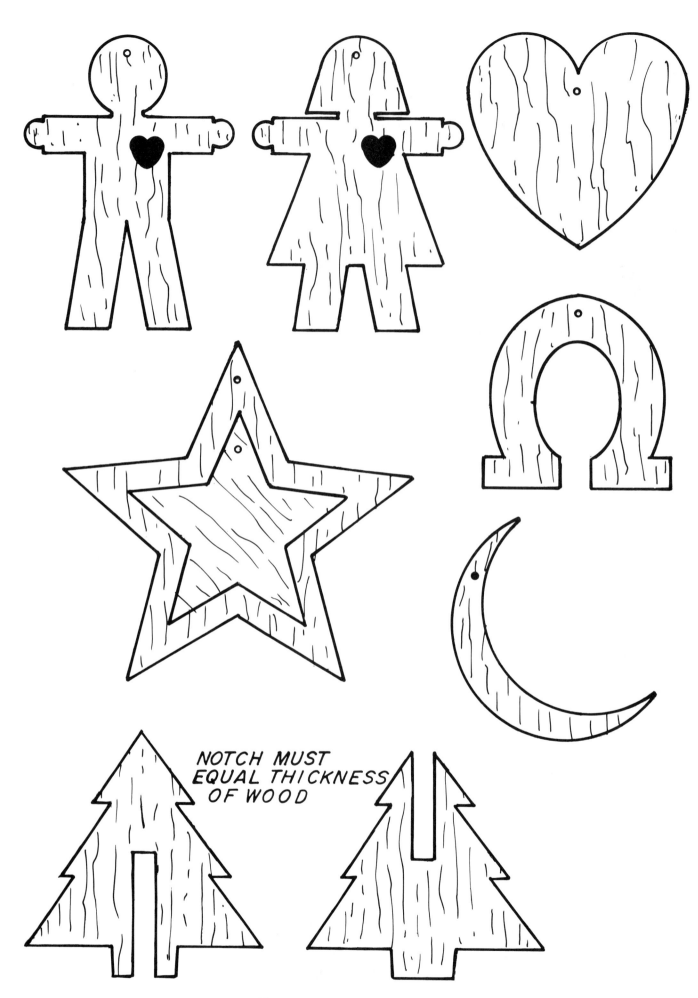

NOTCH MUST
EQUAL THICKNESS
OF WOOD

41

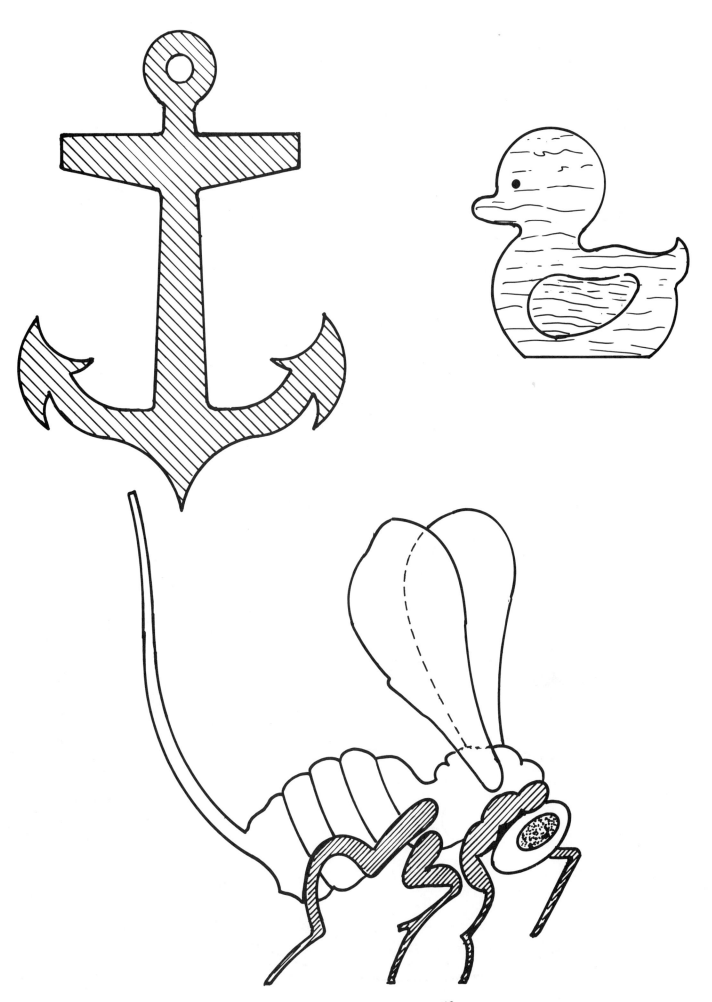

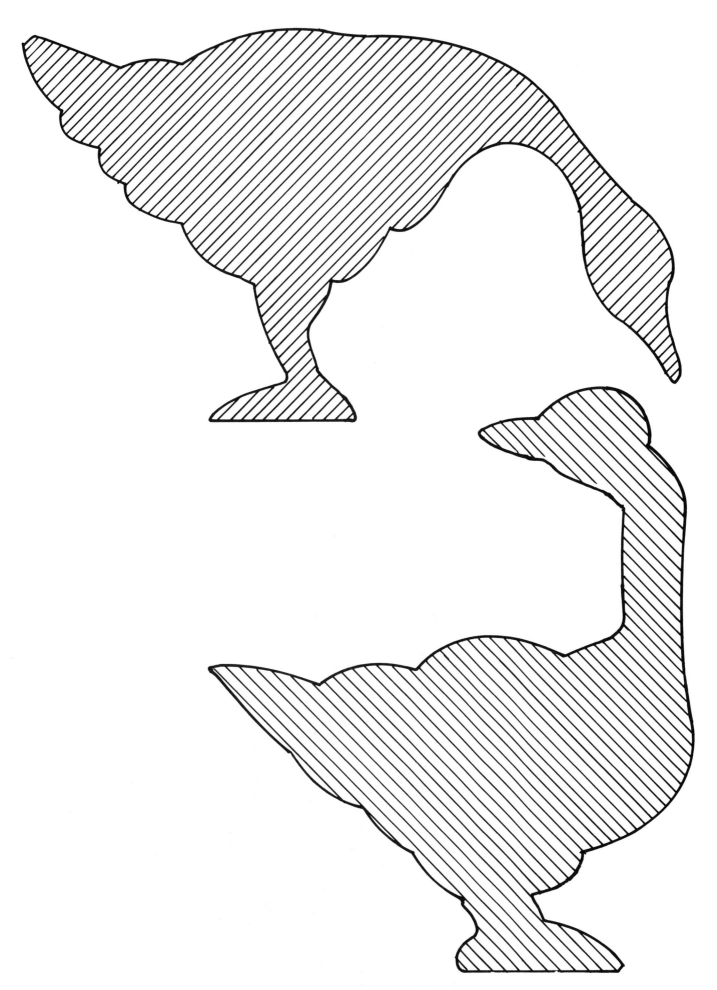

45

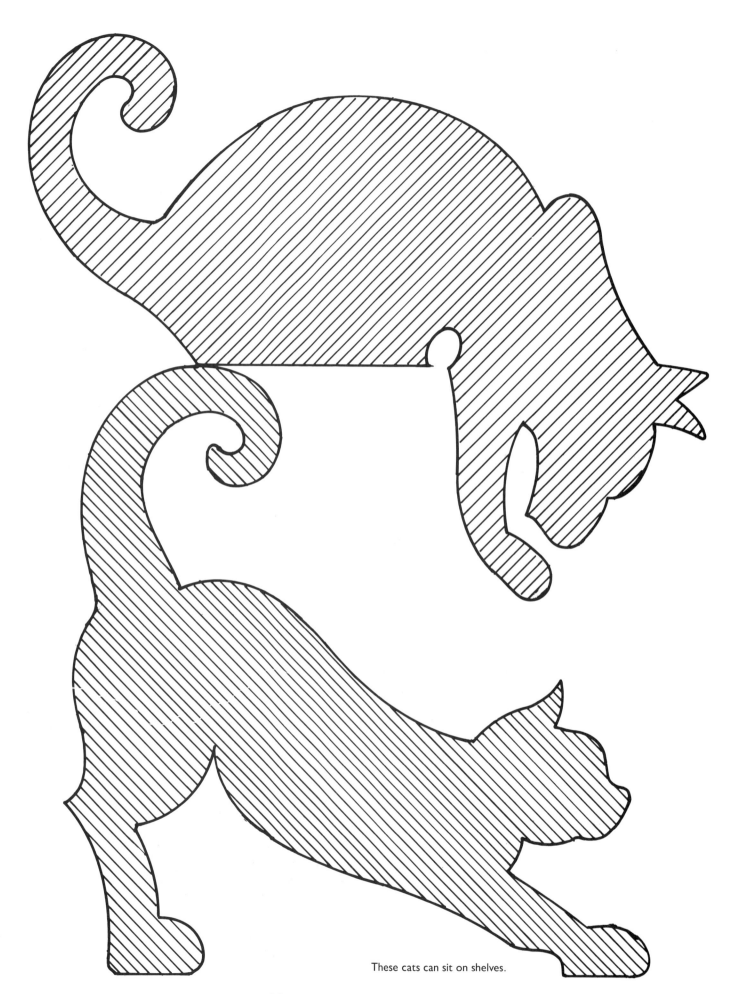

These cats can sit on shelves.

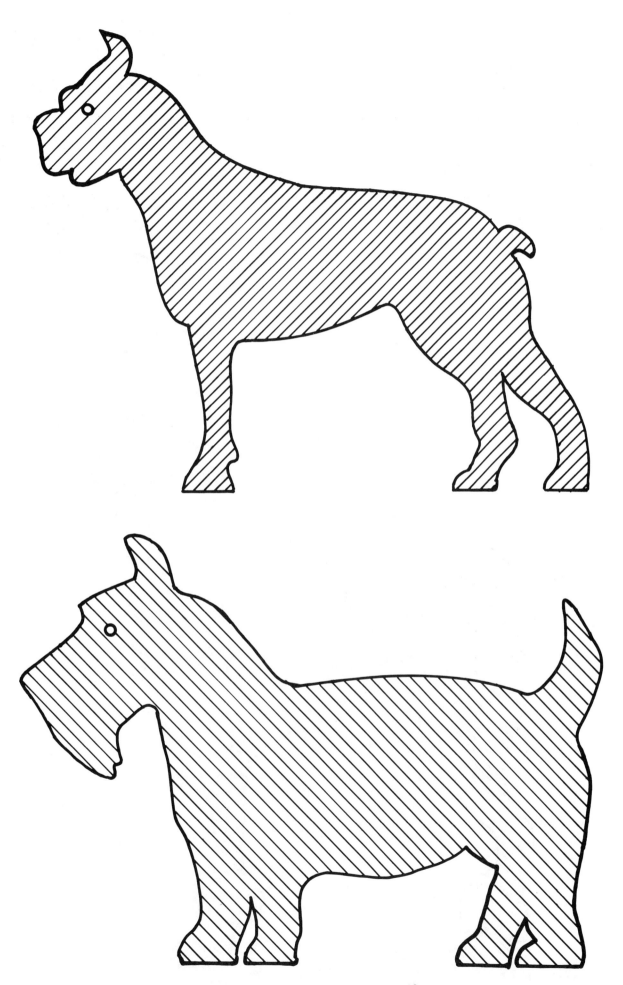

ABCDEFGHIJ
KLMNOPQRS
TUVWXYZ

1234567890

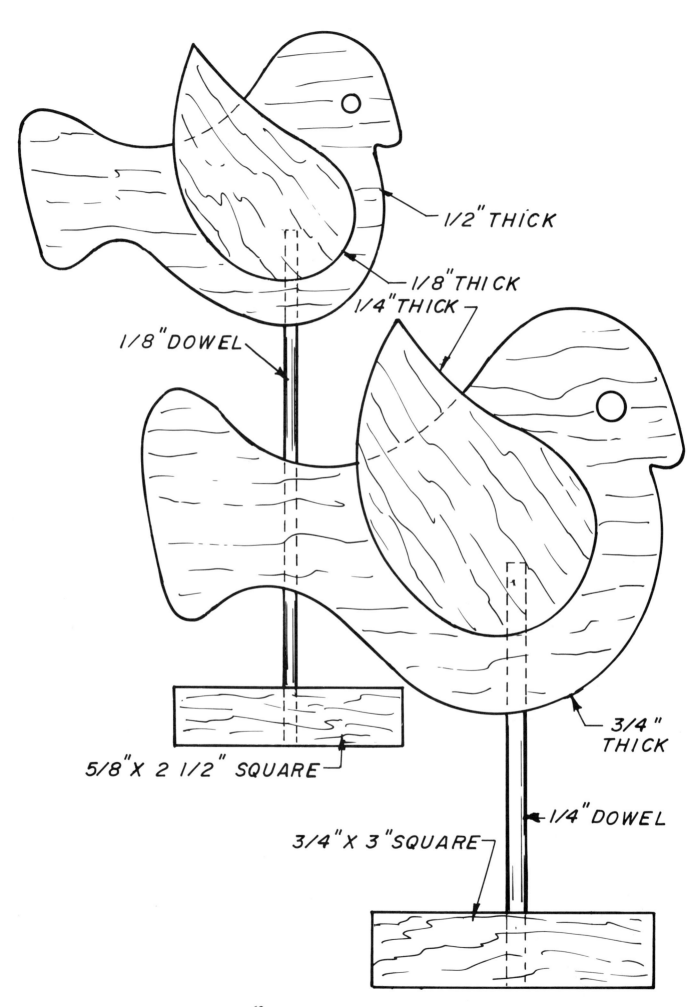

1/2" THICK

1/8" THICK

1/4" THICK

1/8" DOWEL

5/8" X 2 1/2" SQUARE

3/4" THICK

3/4" X 3" SQUARE

1/4" DOWEL

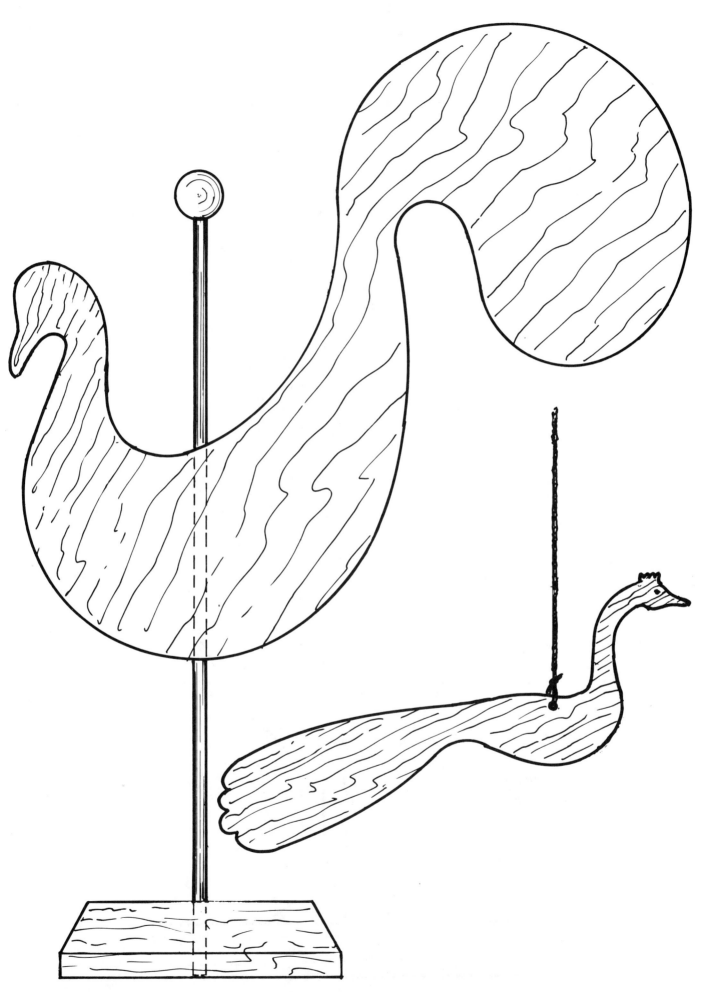

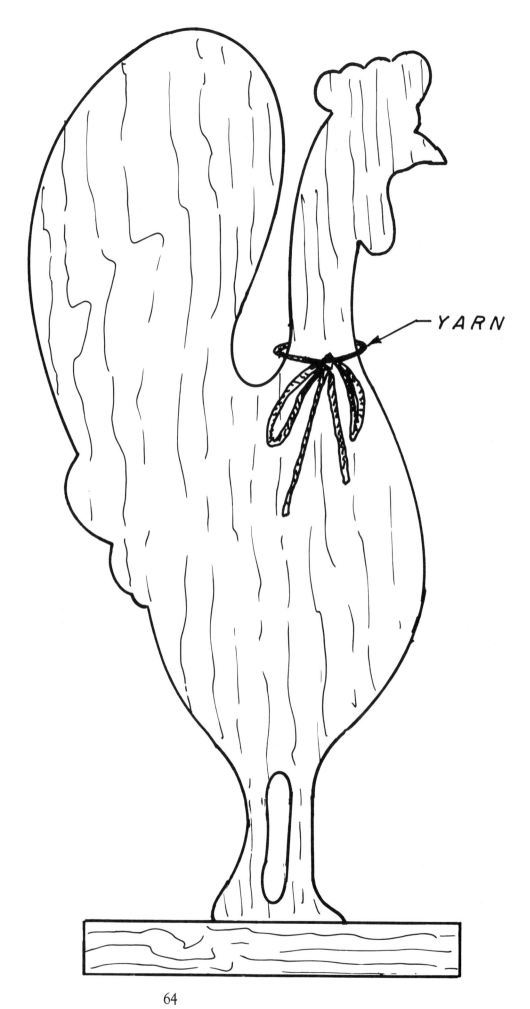

YARN

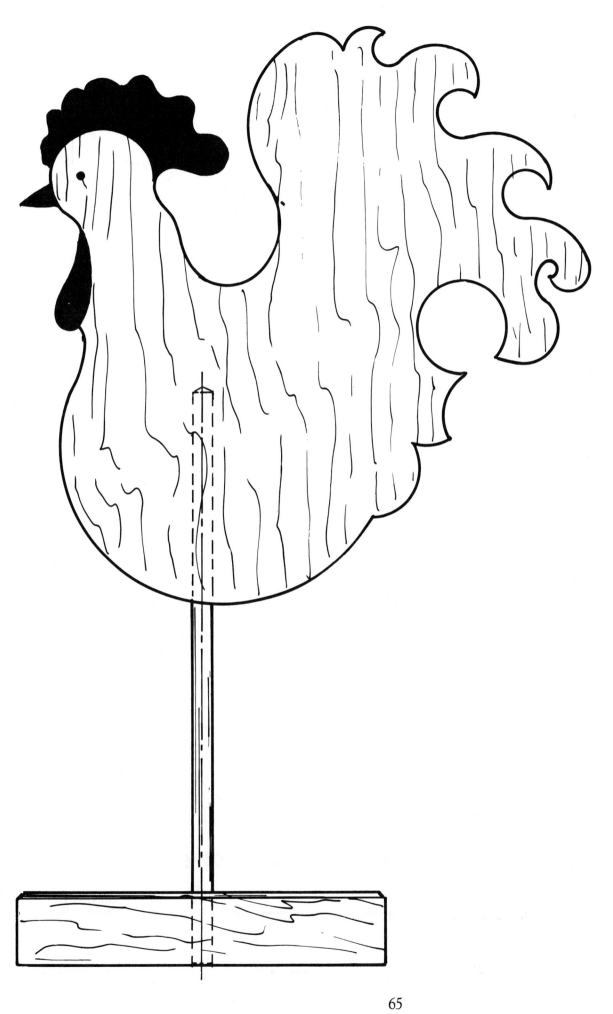

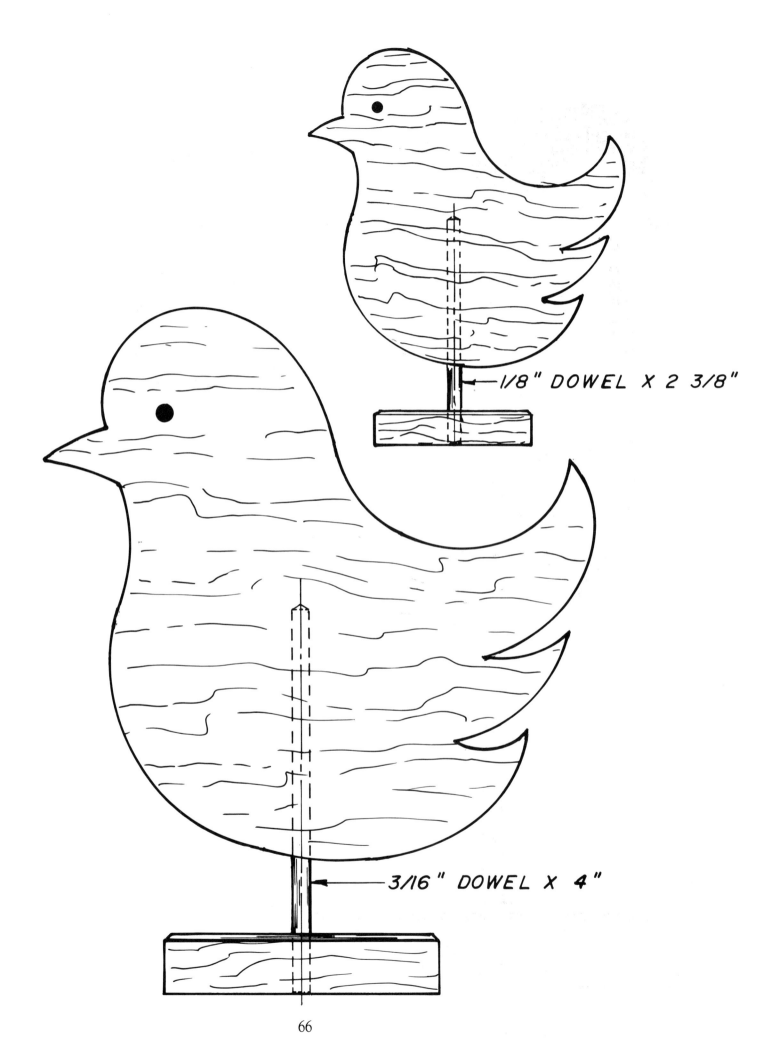

1/8" DOWEL X 2 3/8"

3/16" DOWEL X 4"

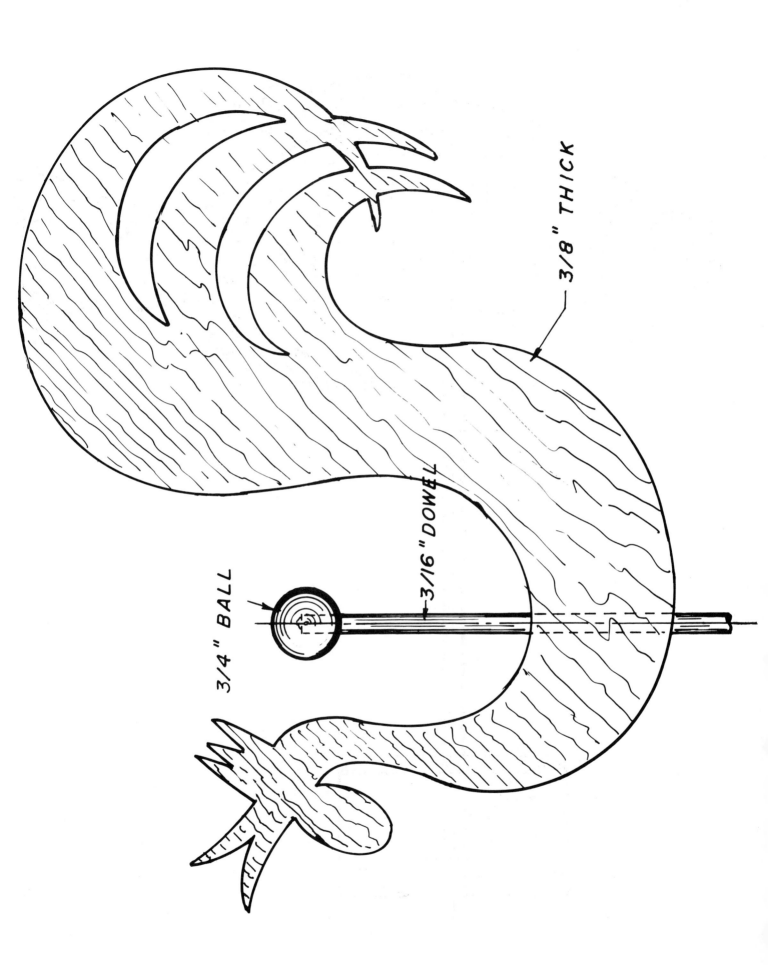

3/8" THICK

3/4" BALL

3/16" DOWEL

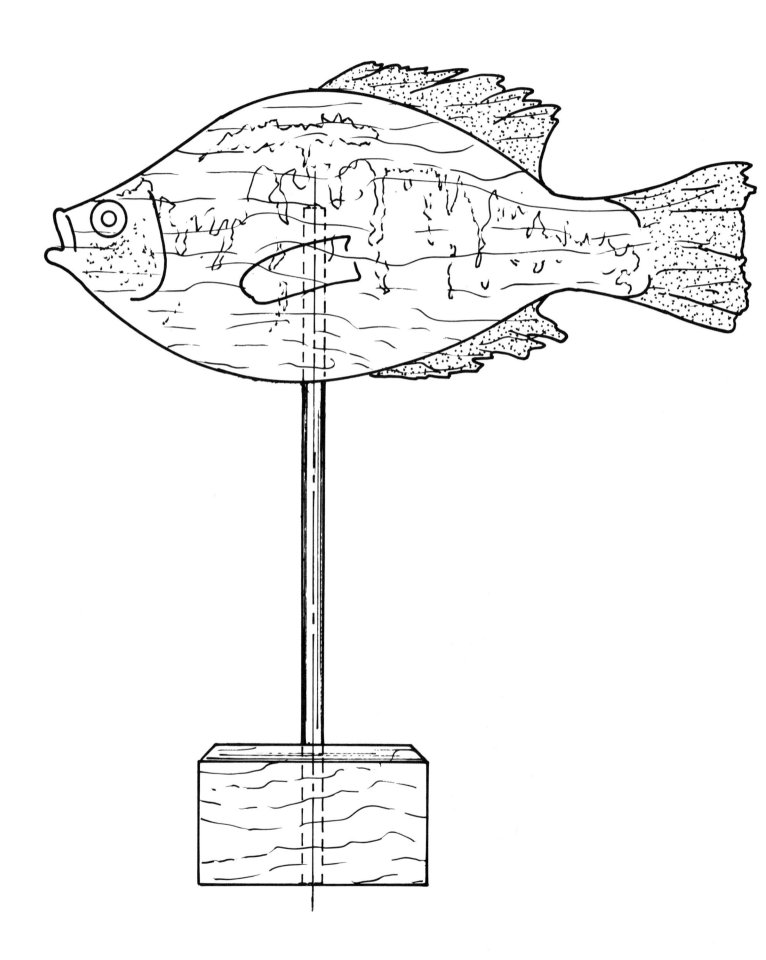

1/4"THICK

3/32" ROD

5/8" X 2" X 4$\frac{1}{2}$"

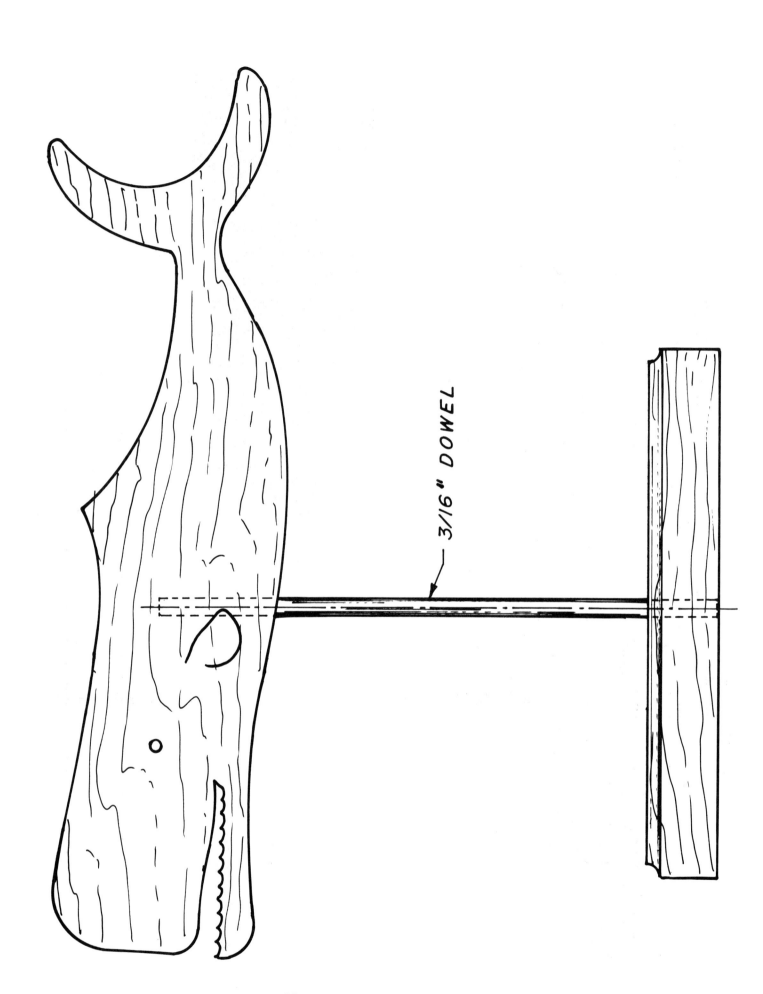

3/16" DOWEL

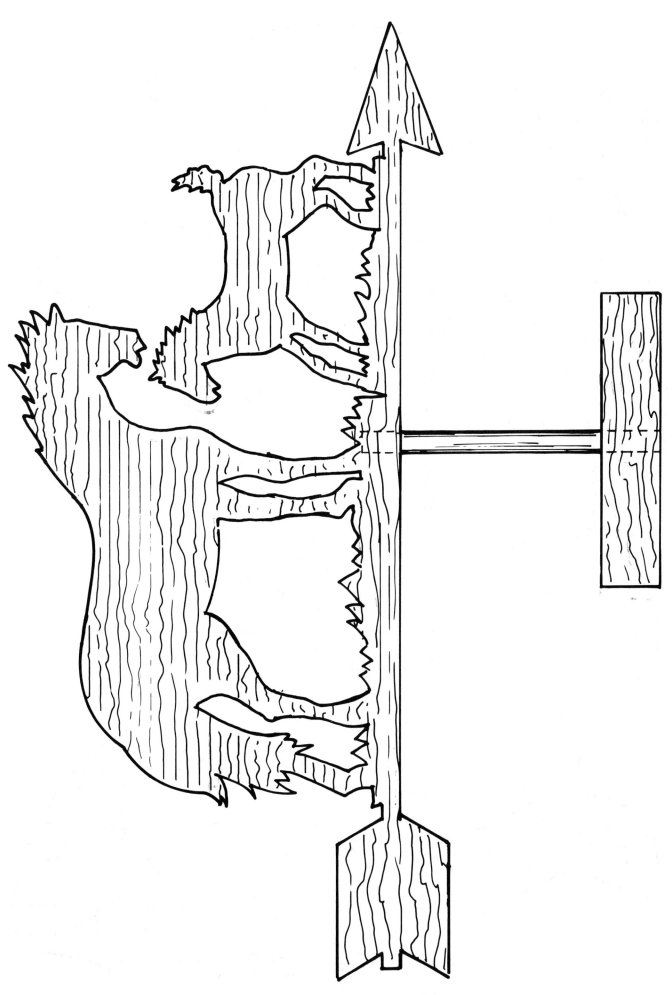

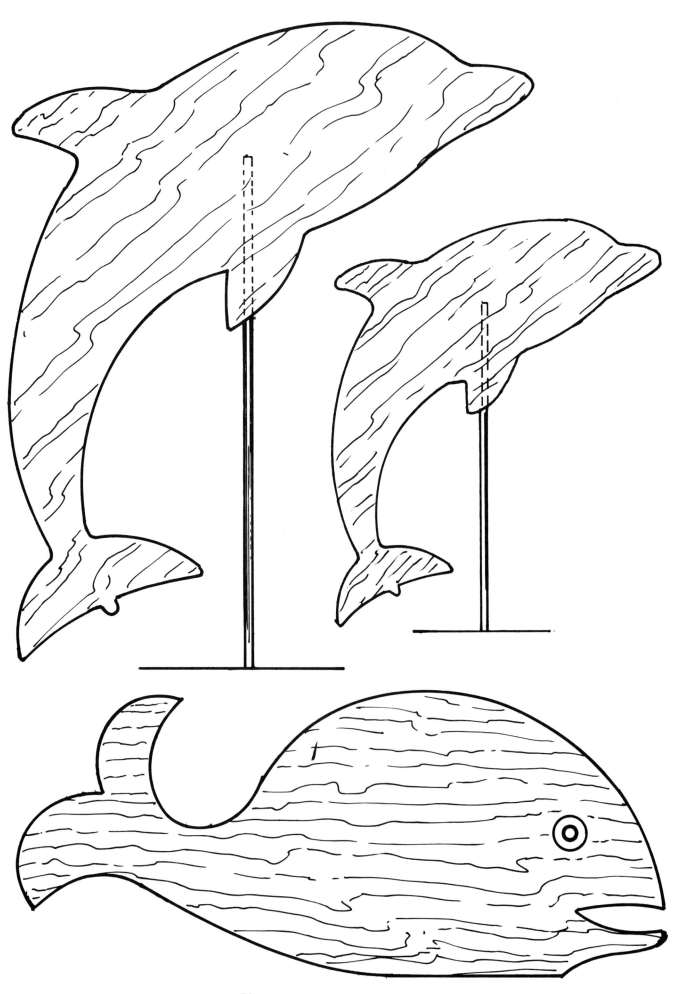

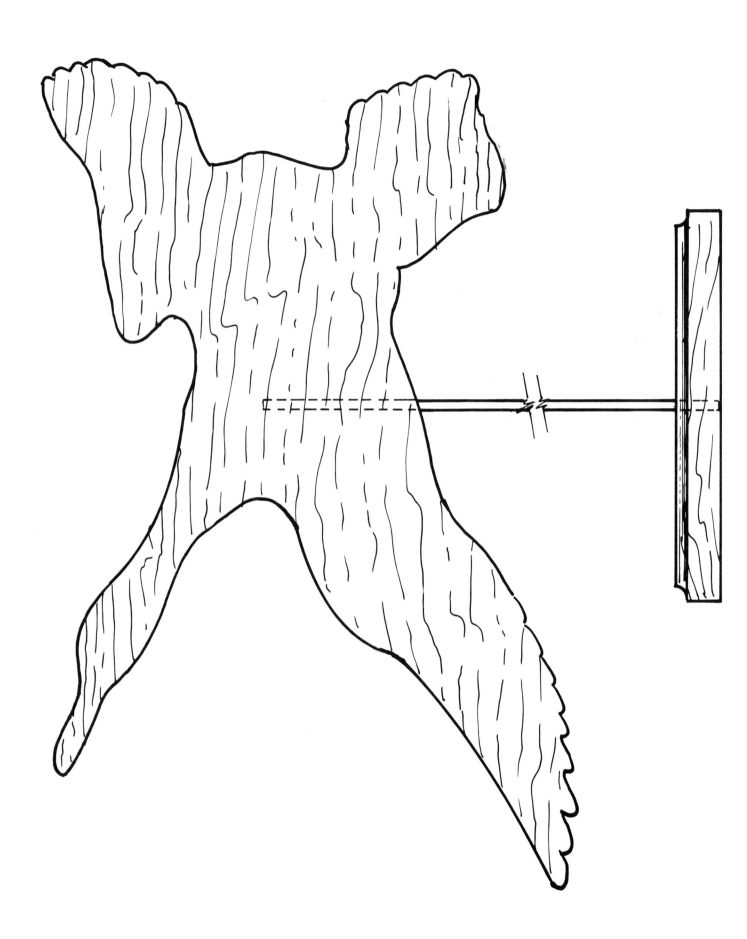

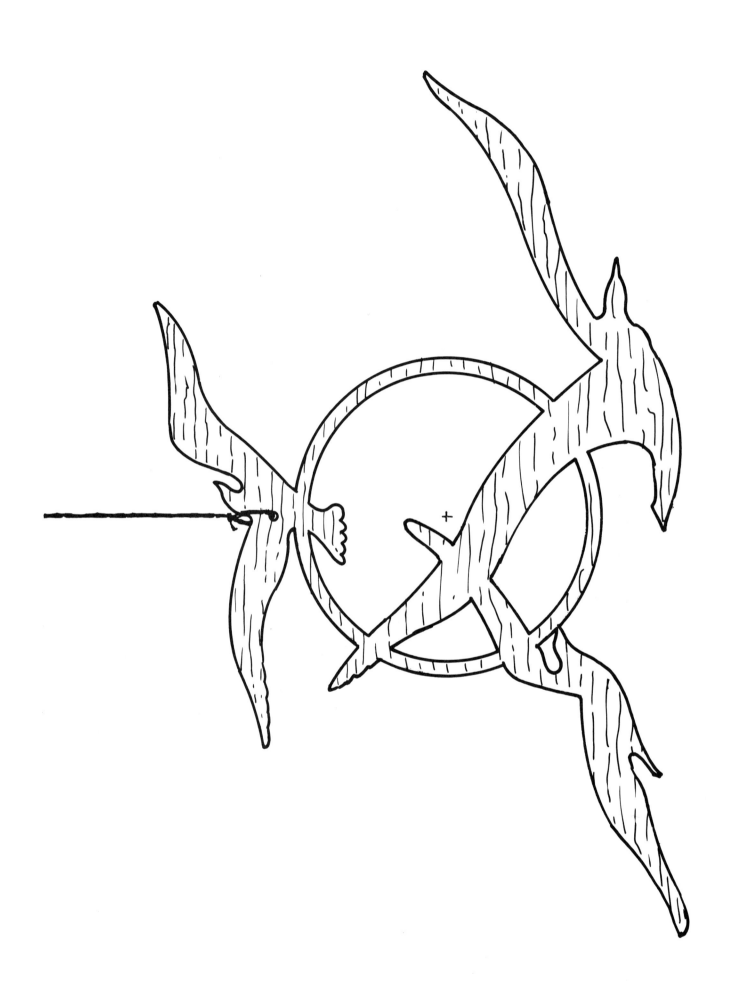

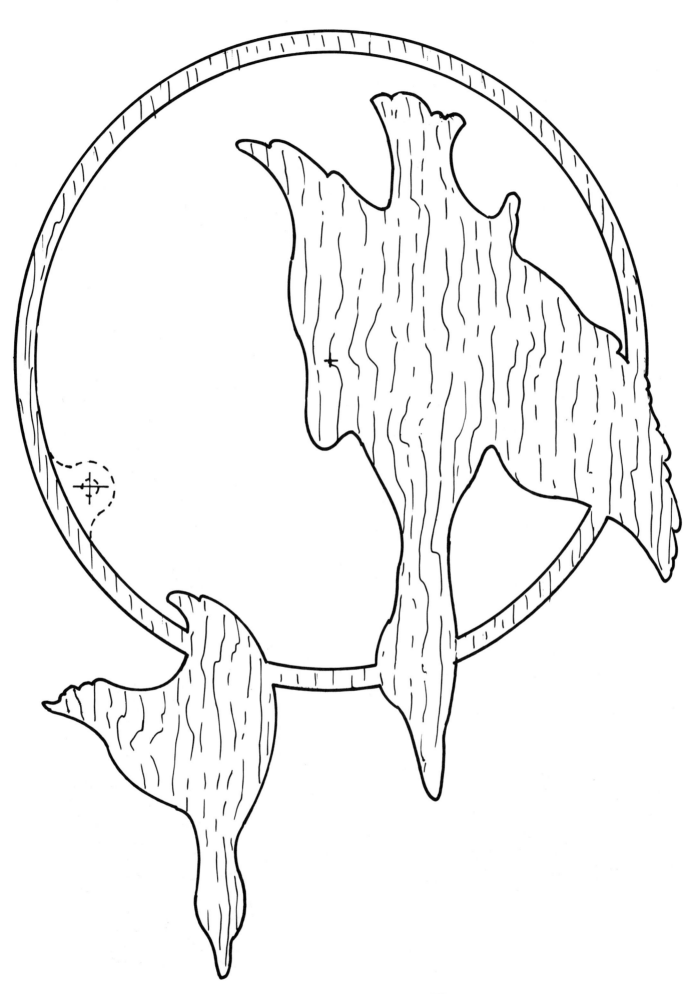

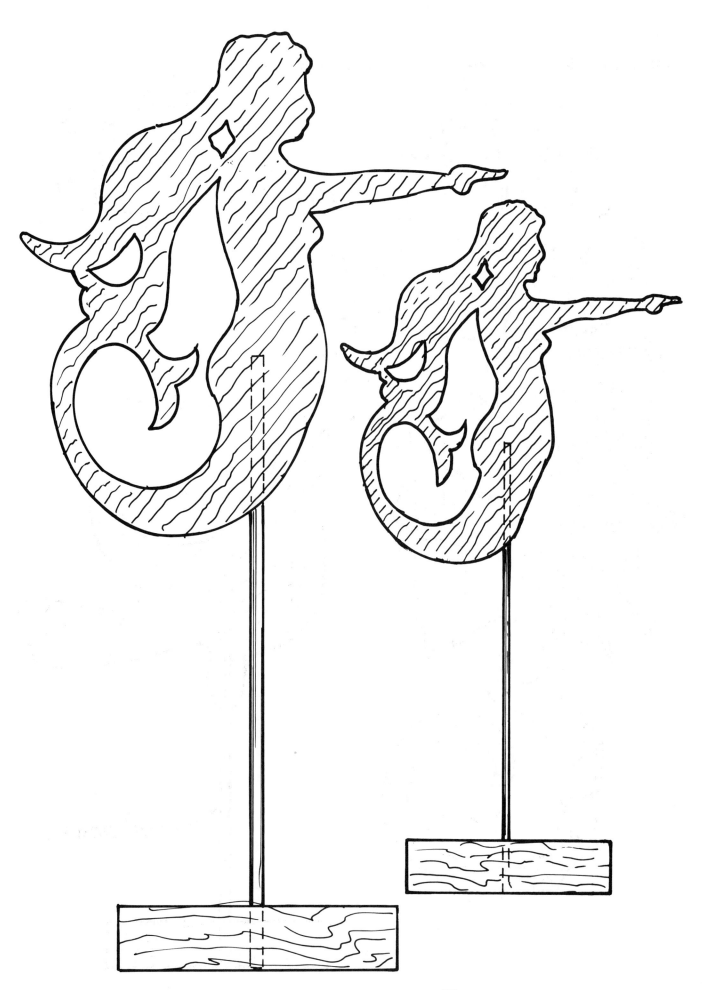

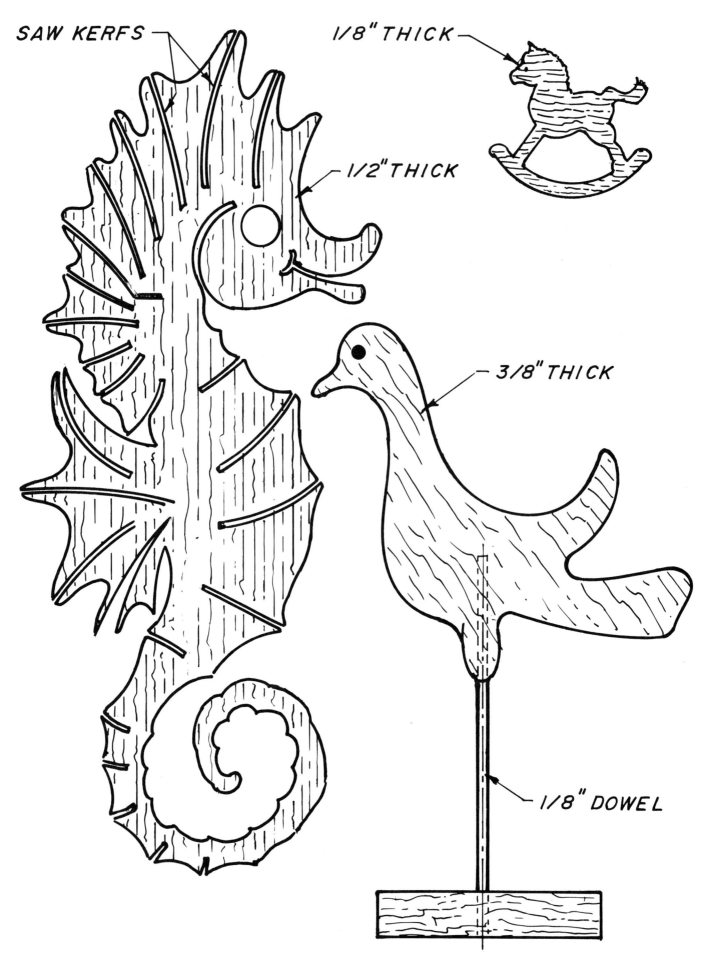

SAW KERFS

1/8" THICK

1/2" THICK

3/8" THICK

1/8" DOWEL

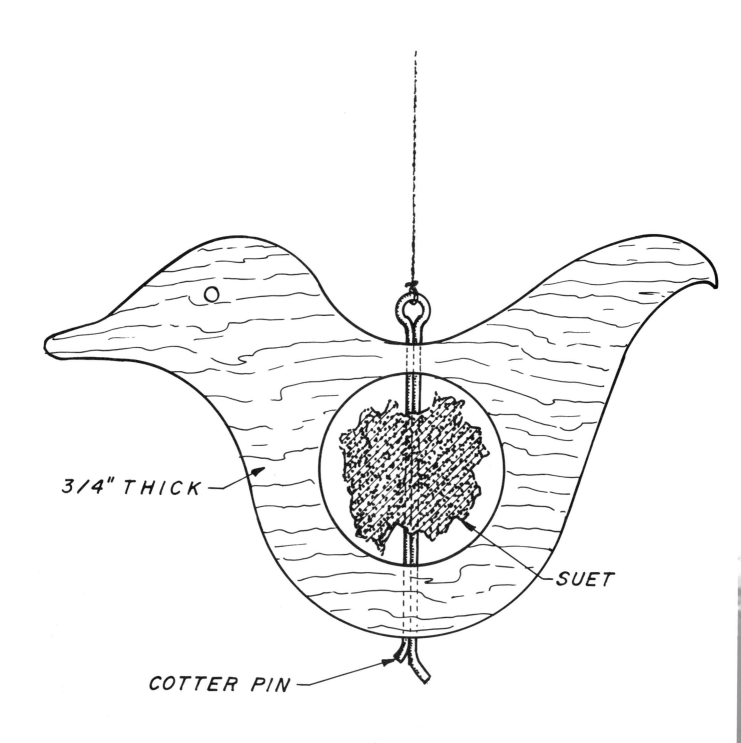

3/4" THICK

SUET

COTTER PIN

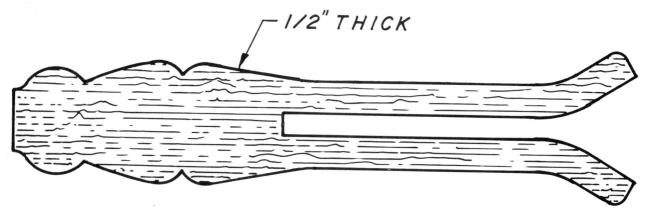

1/2" THICK

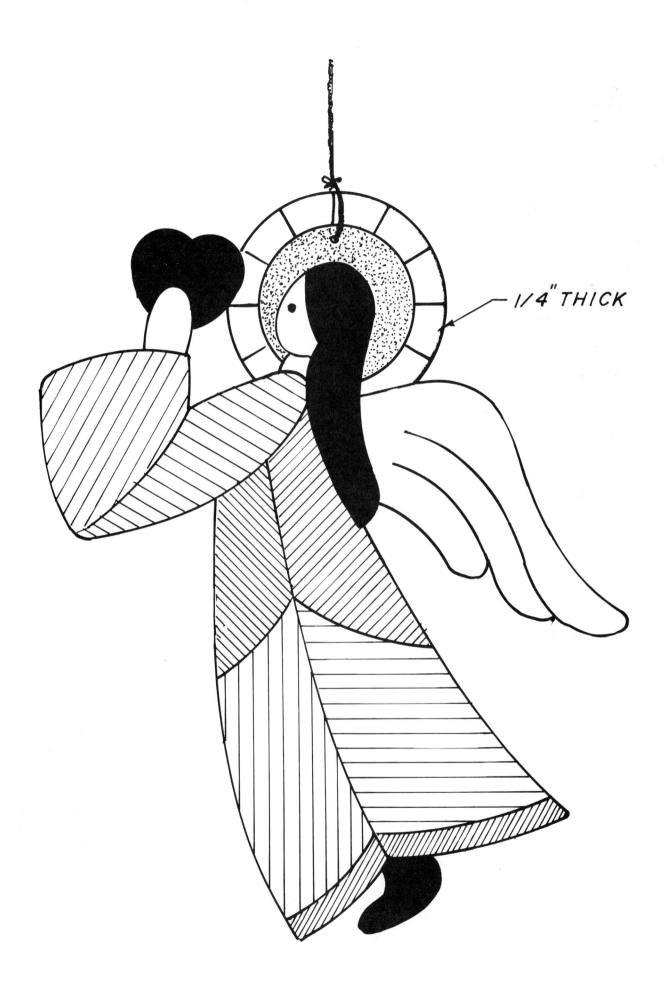

1/4" THICK

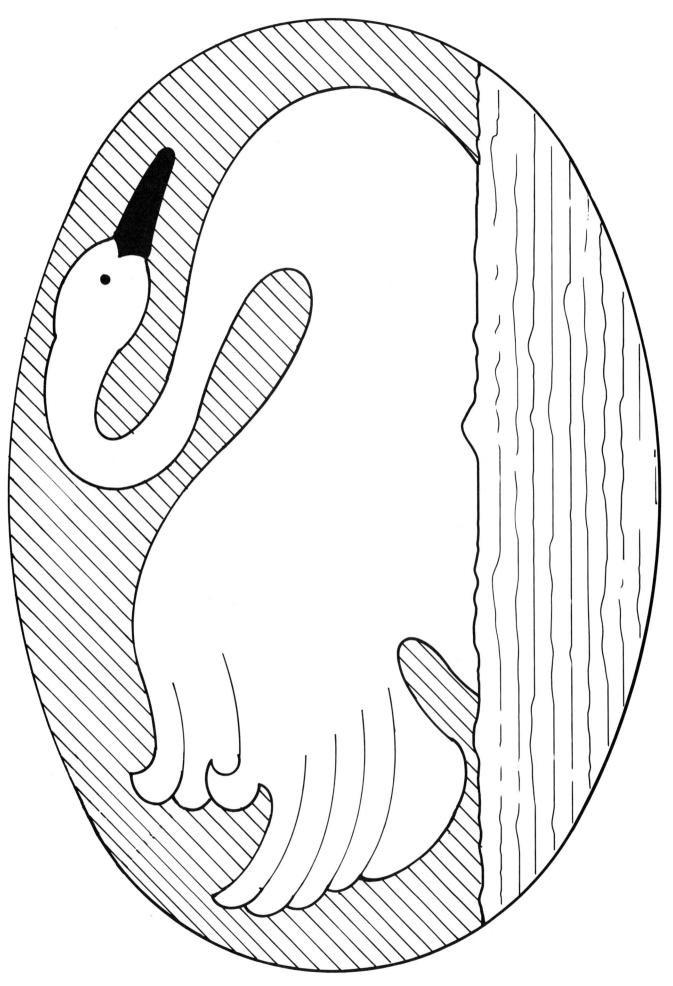

85

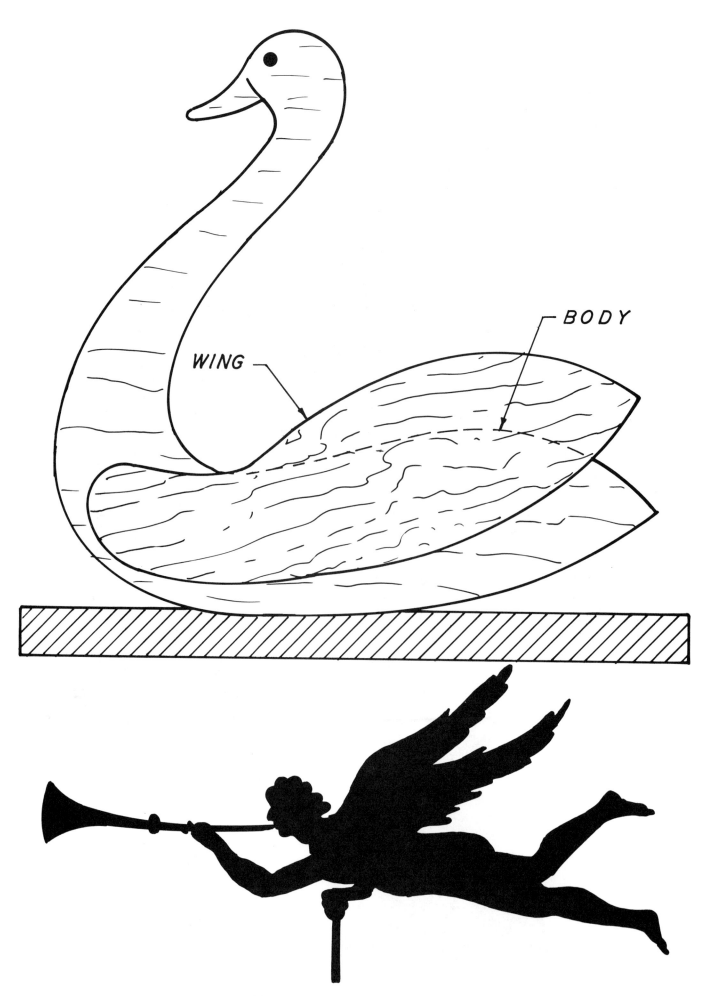

WING

BODY

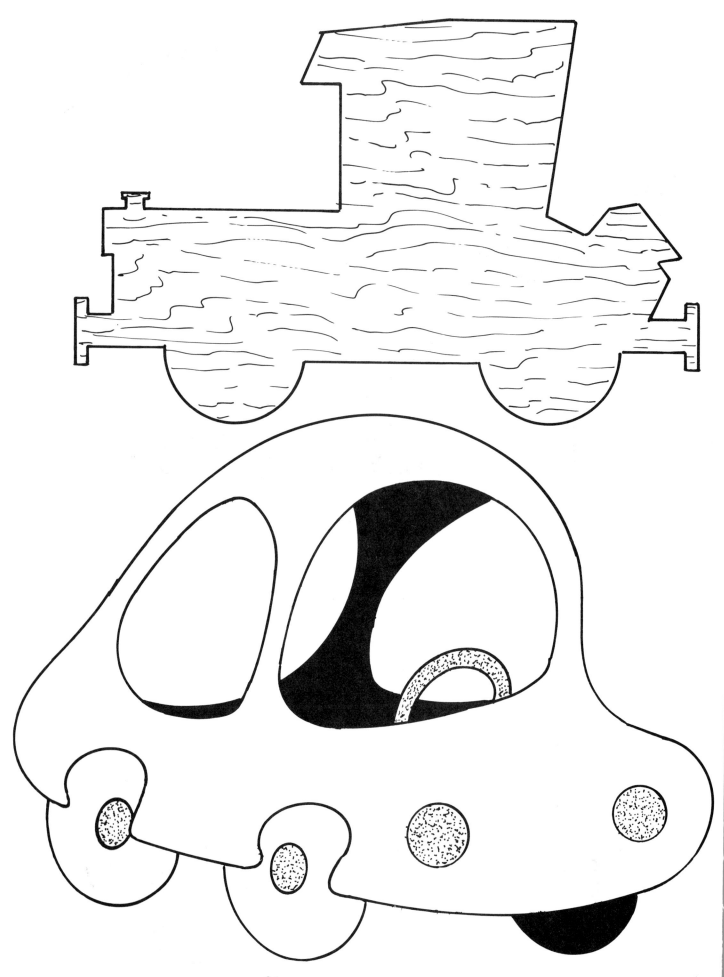

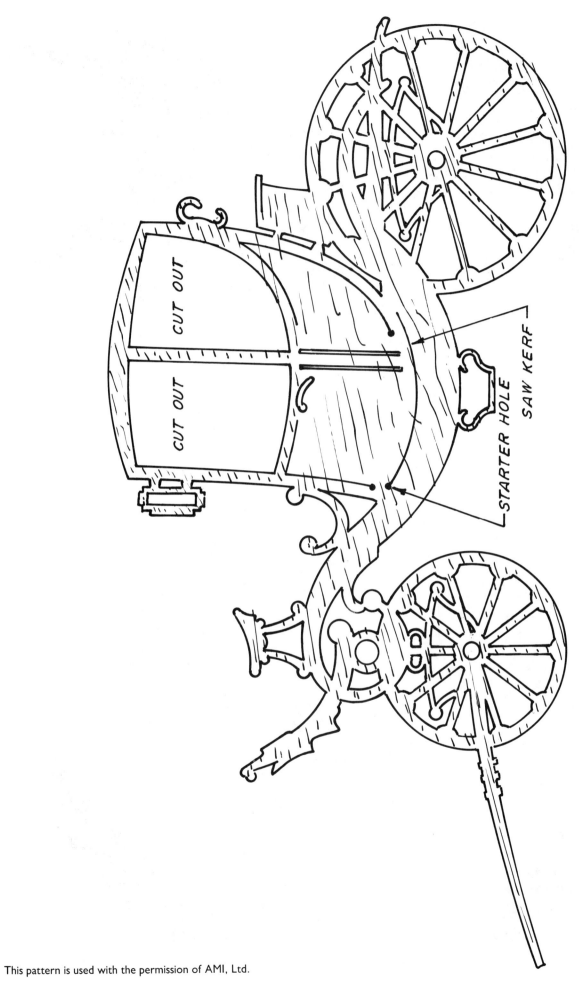

CUT OUT CUT OUT

CUT OUT

STARTER HOLE

SAW KERF

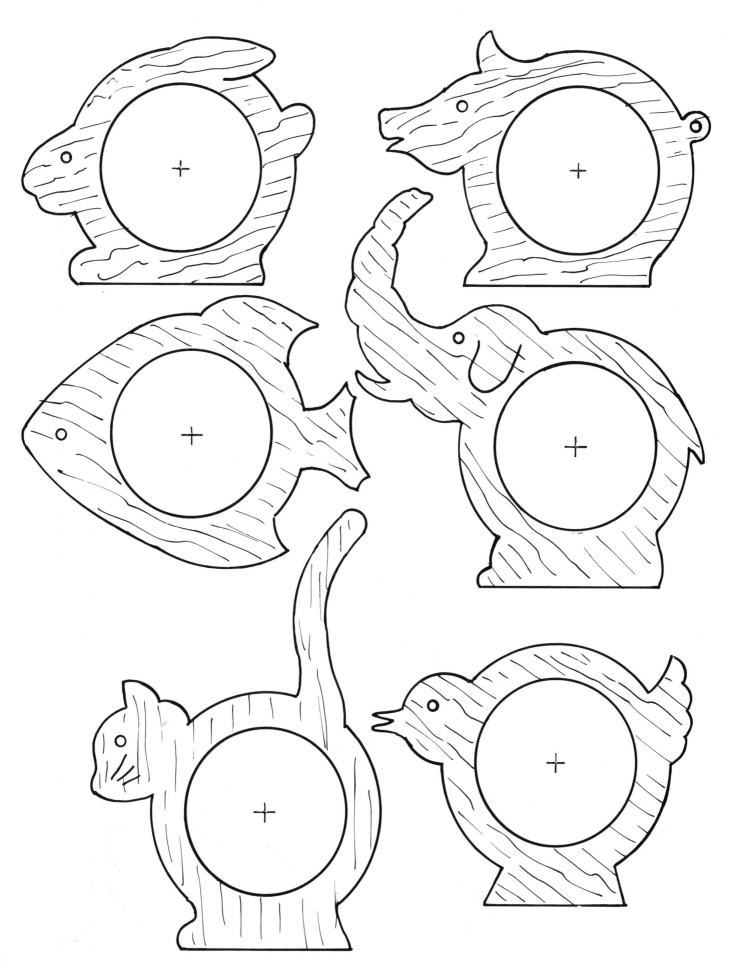

1/8" THICK

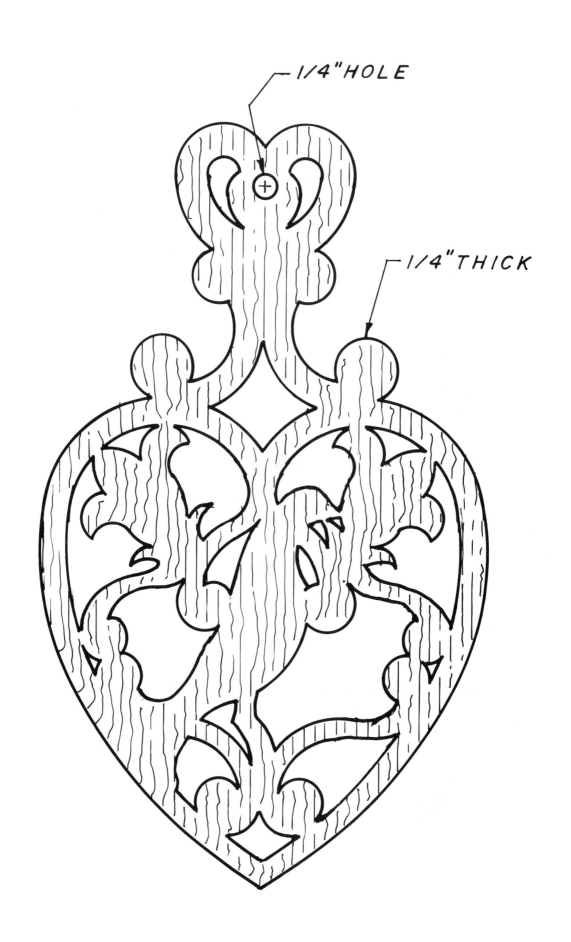

1/4"HOLE

1/4"THICK

Locate and drill twelve 1¼-inch holes before cutting out
the rest of the pattern.

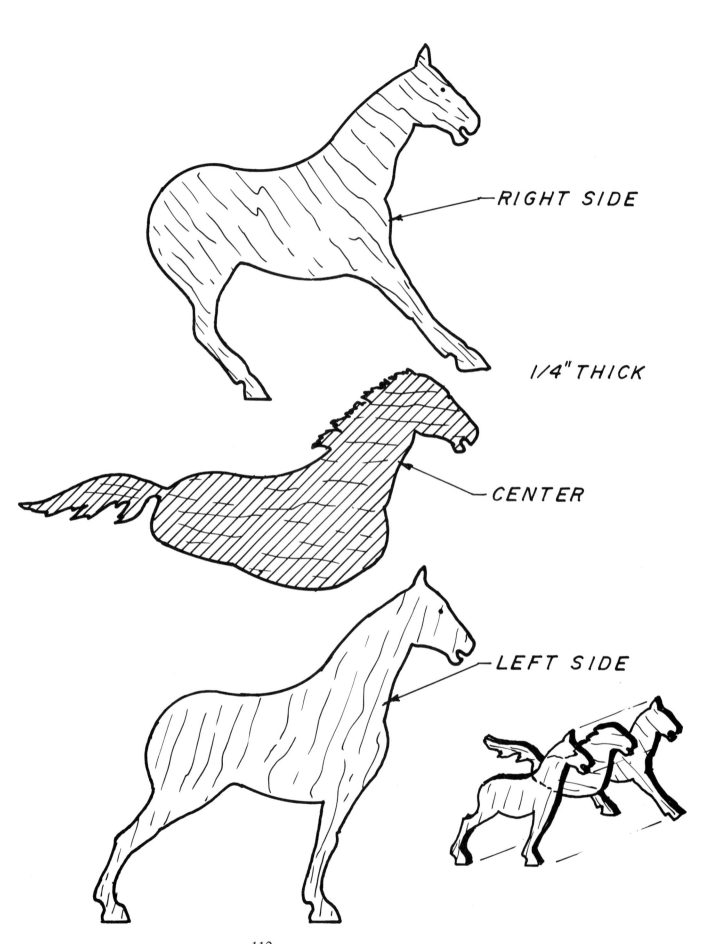

RIGHT SIDE

1/4" THICK

CENTER

LEFT SIDE

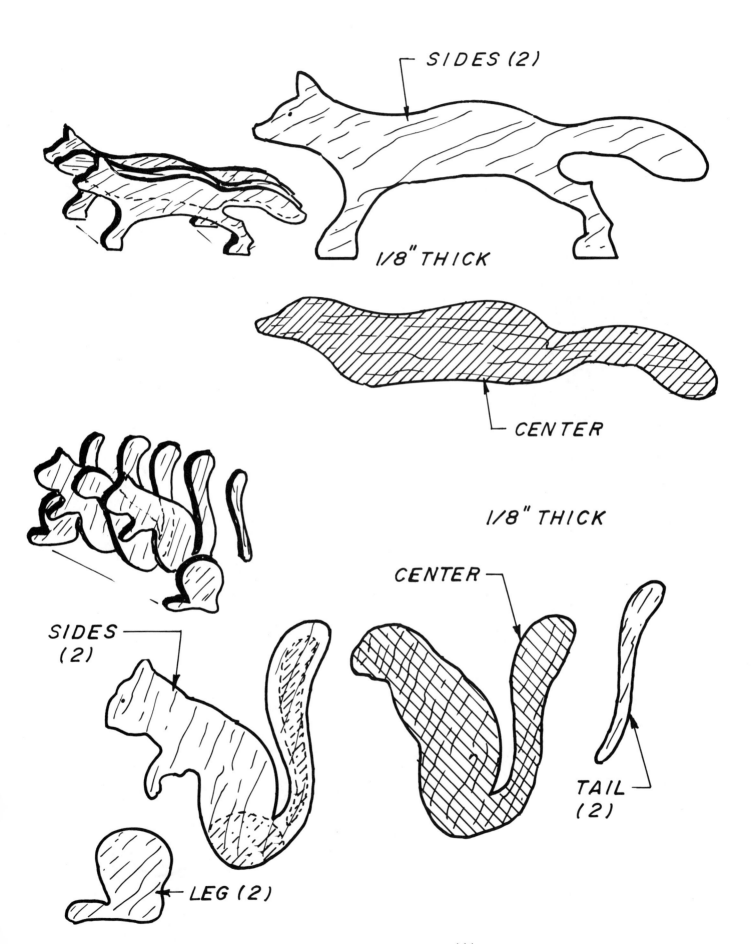

SIDES (2)

1/8" THICK

CENTER

1/8" THICK

CENTER

SIDES
(2)

TAIL
(2)

LEG (2)

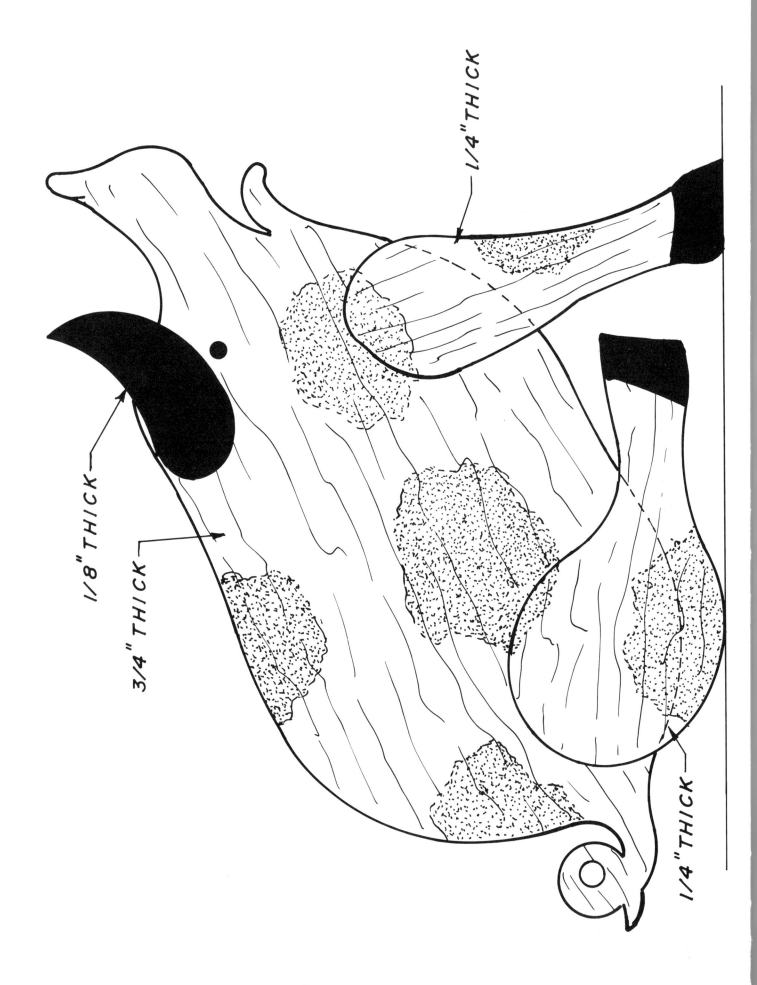

1/4" THICK

1/8" THICK

3/4" THICK

1/4" THICK

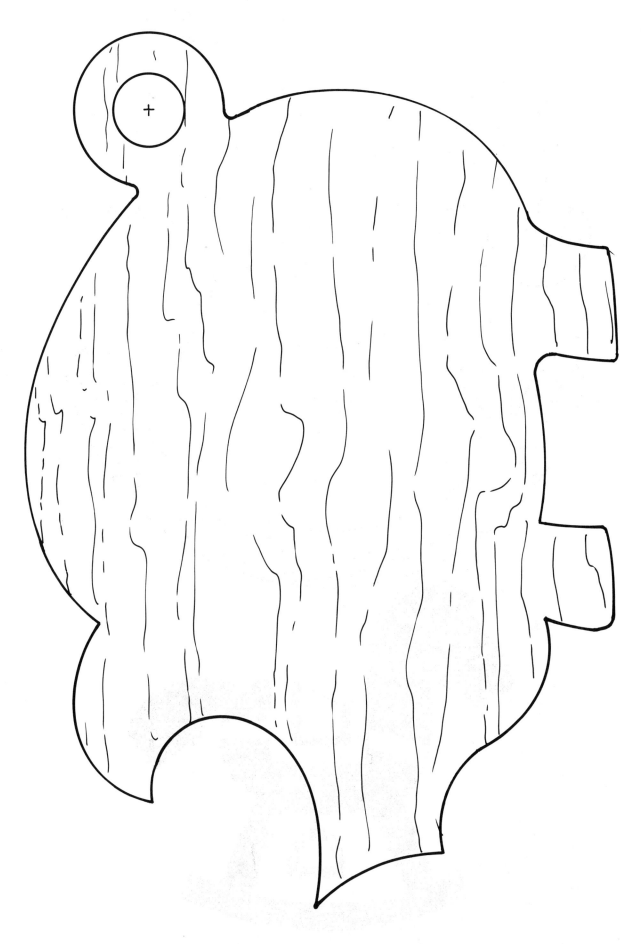

3/8" THICK

114

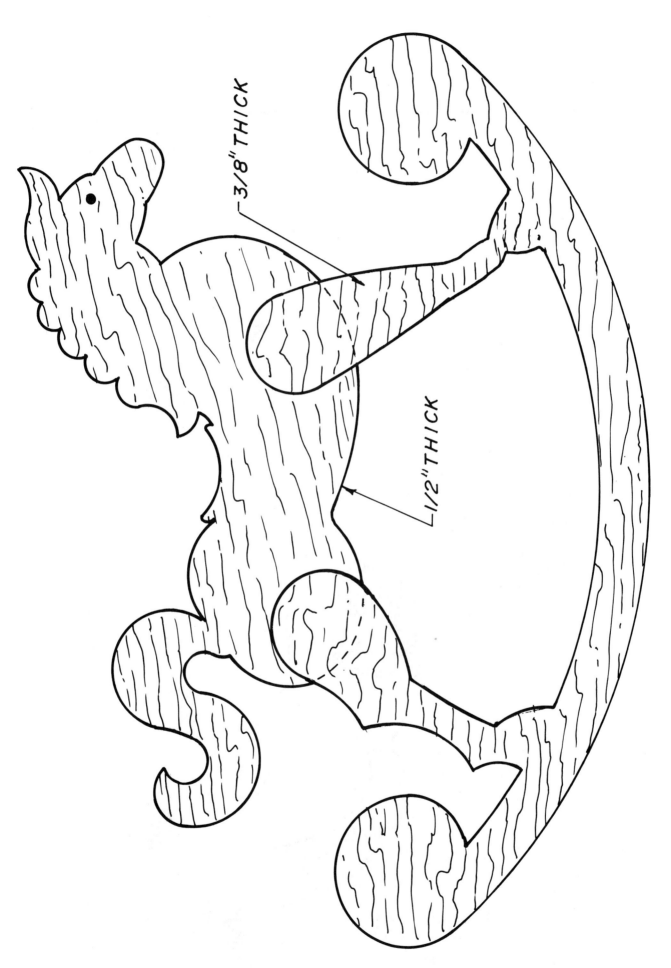

3/8" THICK

1/2" THICK

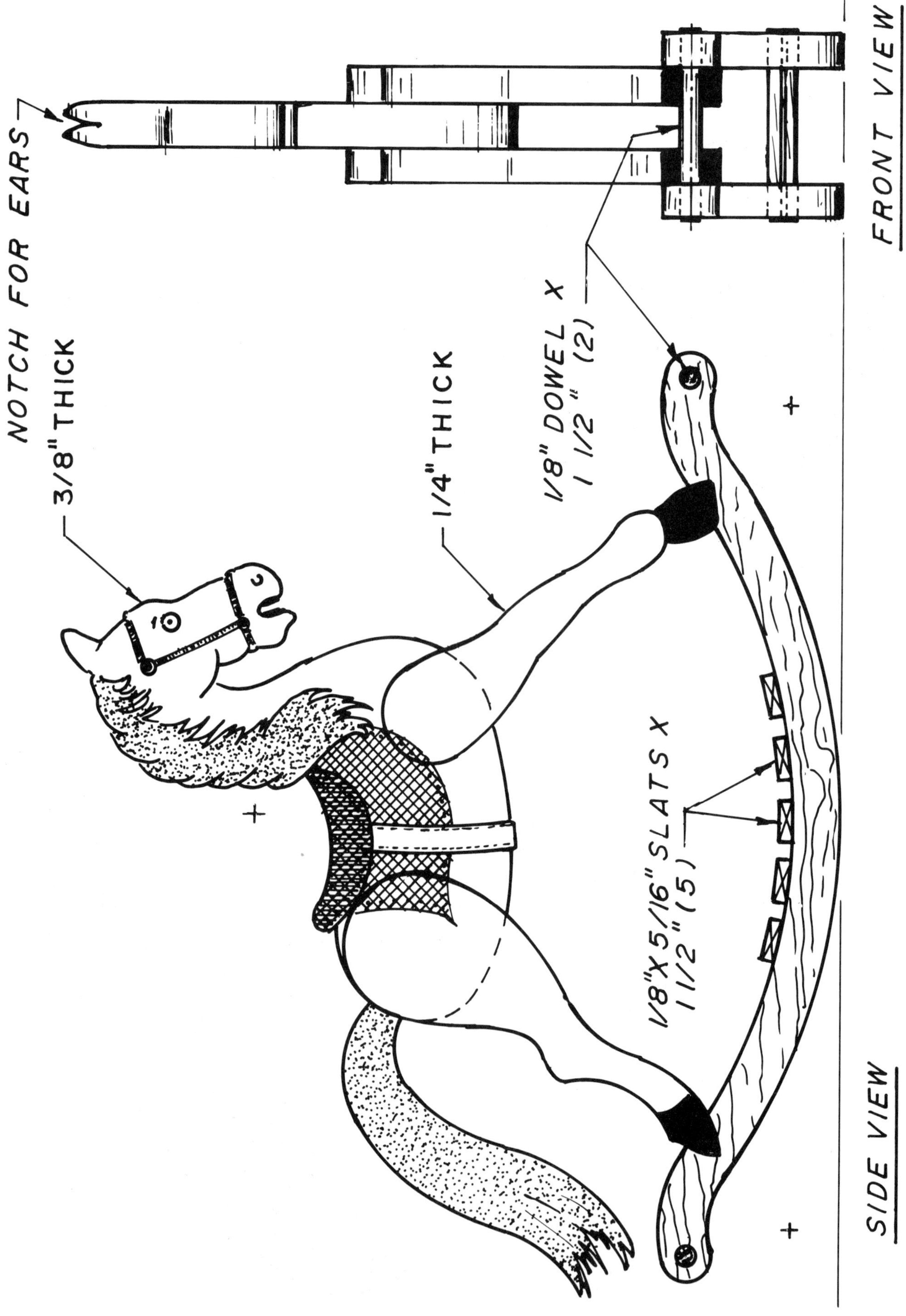

NOTCH FOR EARS

3/8" THICK

1/4" THICK

1/8" DOWEL X
1 1/2" (2)

1/8" X 5/16" SLATS X
1 1/2" (5)

FRONT VIEW

SIDE VIEW

116

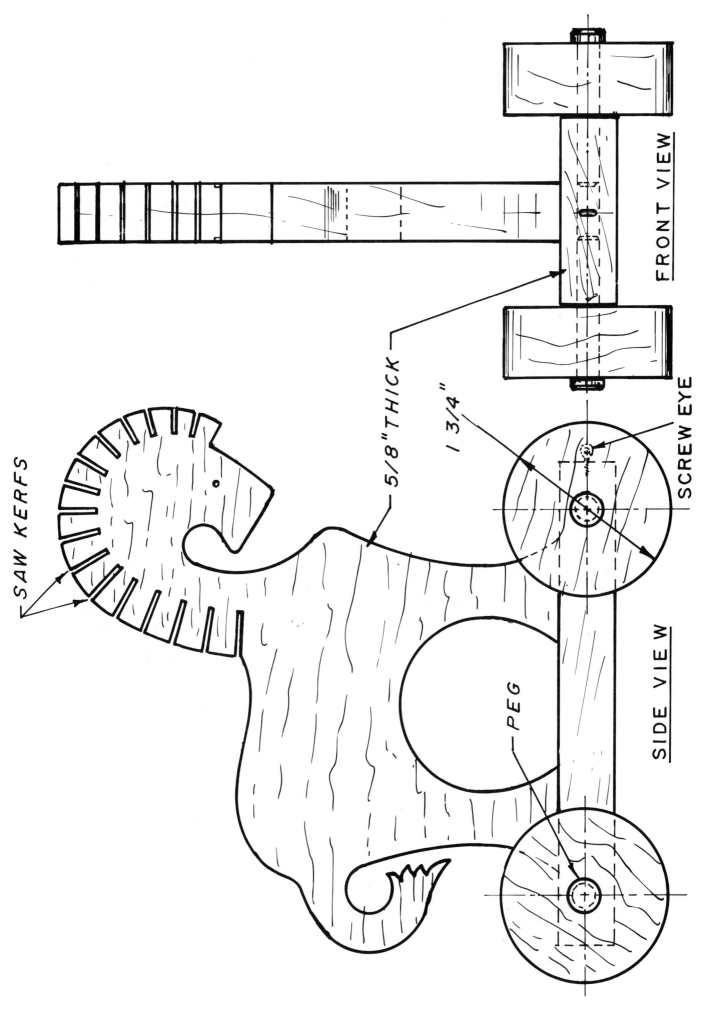

SAW KERFS

FRONT VIEW

5/8" THICK

1 3/4"

SCREW EYE

PEG

SIDE VIEW

117

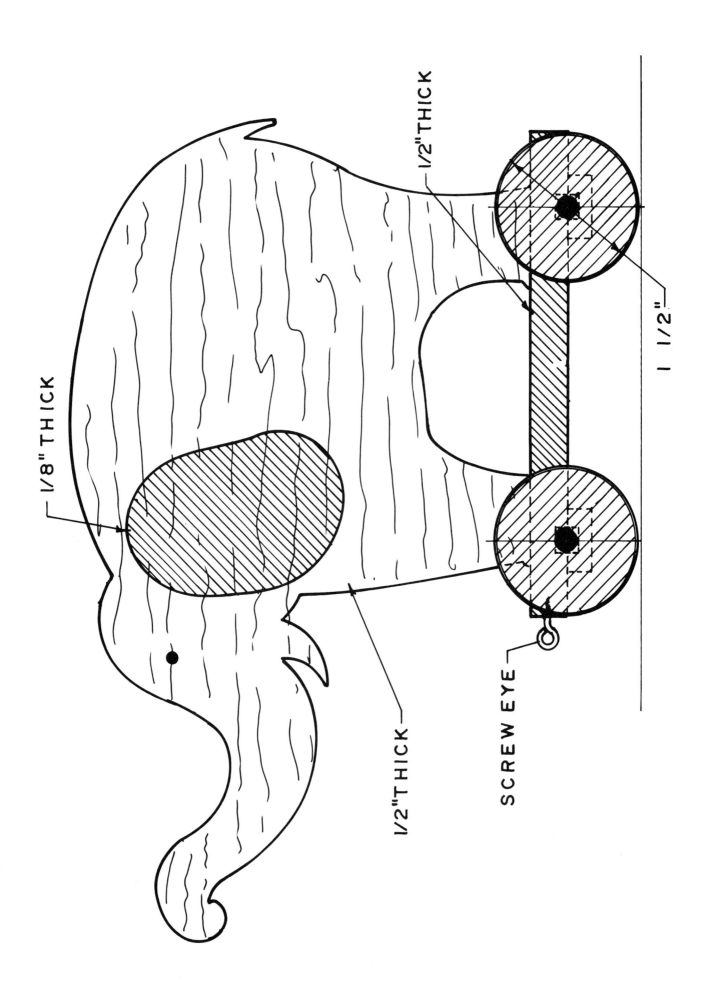

1/2" THICK

1/8" THICK

1/2" THICK

SCREW EYE

1 1/2"

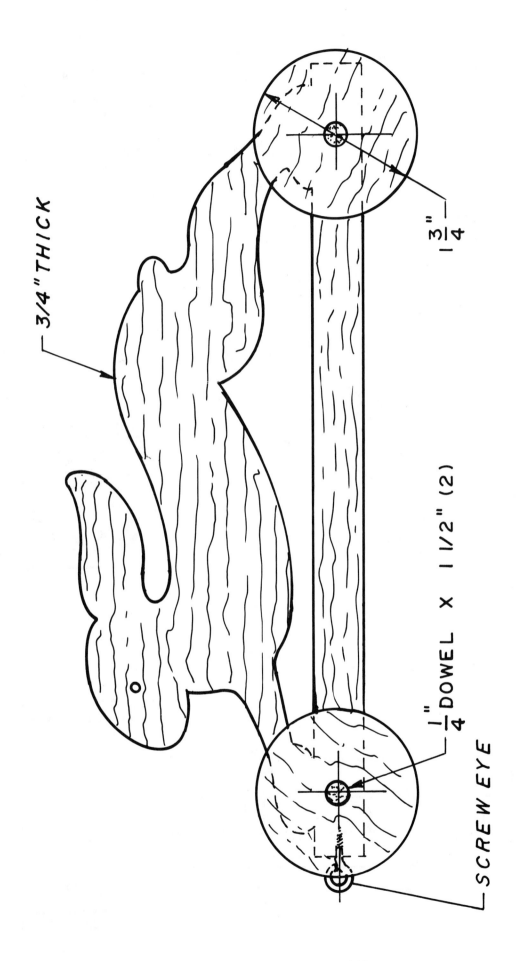

3/4" THICK

$\frac{3}{4}$"

$\frac{1}{4}$" DOWEL X 1 1/2" (2)

SCREW EYE

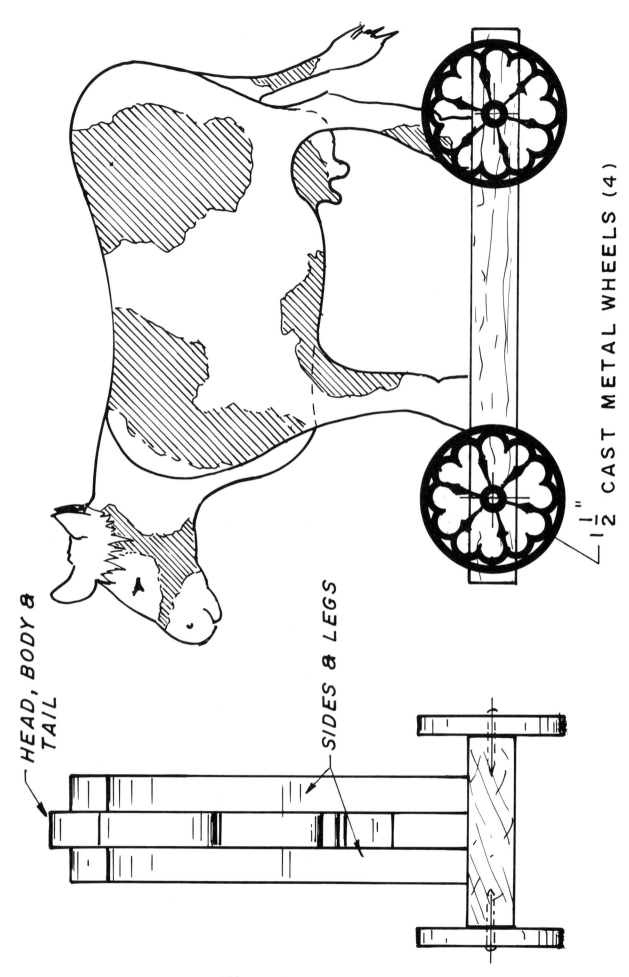

HEAD, BODY & TAIL

SIDES & LEGS

$1\frac{1}{2}$" CAST METAL WHEELS (4)

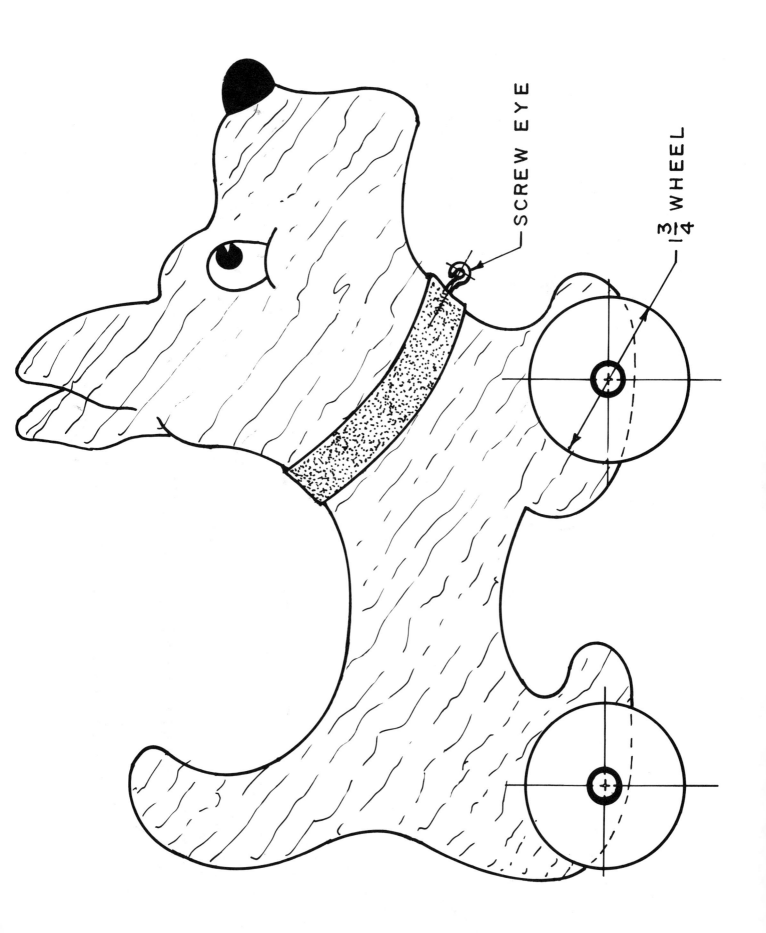

SCREW EYE

$1\frac{3}{4}$ WHEEL

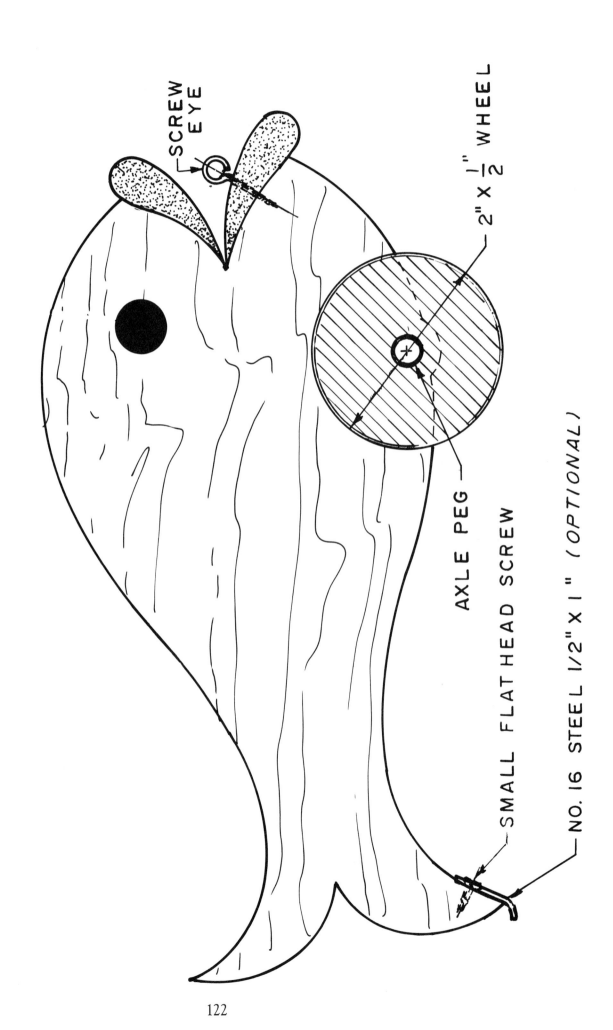

SCREW EYE

2" X $\frac{1}{2}$" WHEEL

AXLE PEG

SMALL FLAT HEAD SCREW

NO. 16 STEEL 1/2" X 1" (OPTIONAL)

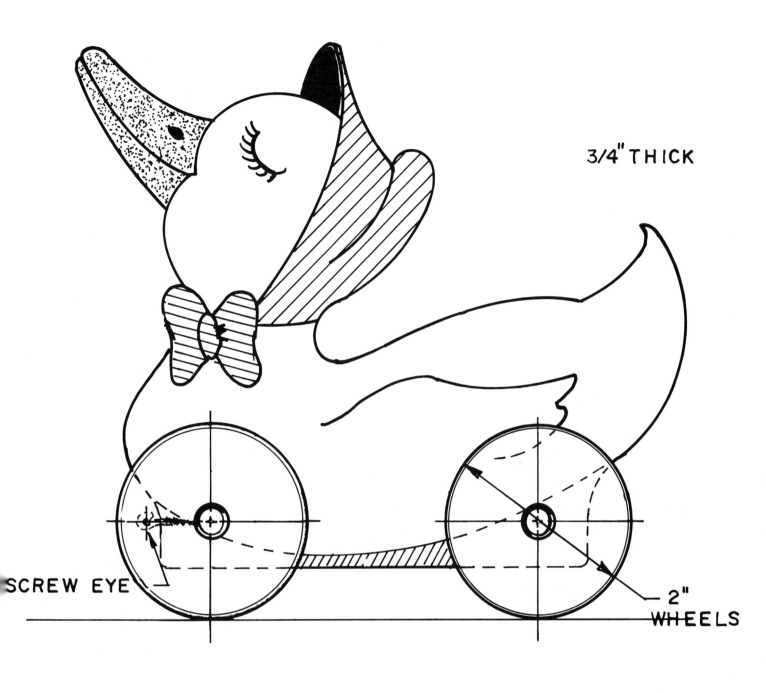

3/4" THICK

SCREW EYE

2" WHEELS

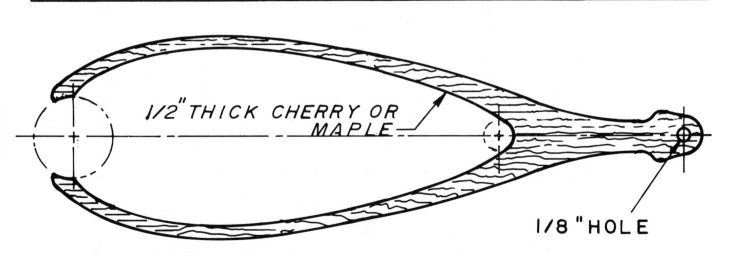

1/2" THICK CHERRY OR MAPLE

1/8" HOLE

123

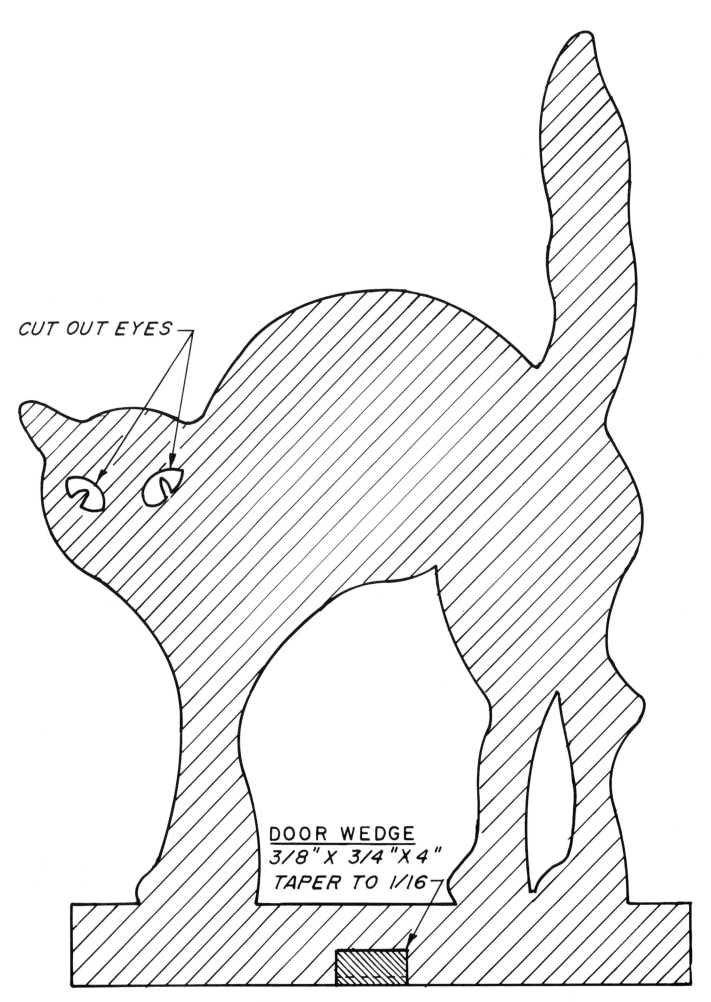

CUT OUT EYES

DOOR WEDGE
3/8" X 3/4" X 4"
TAPER TO 1/16

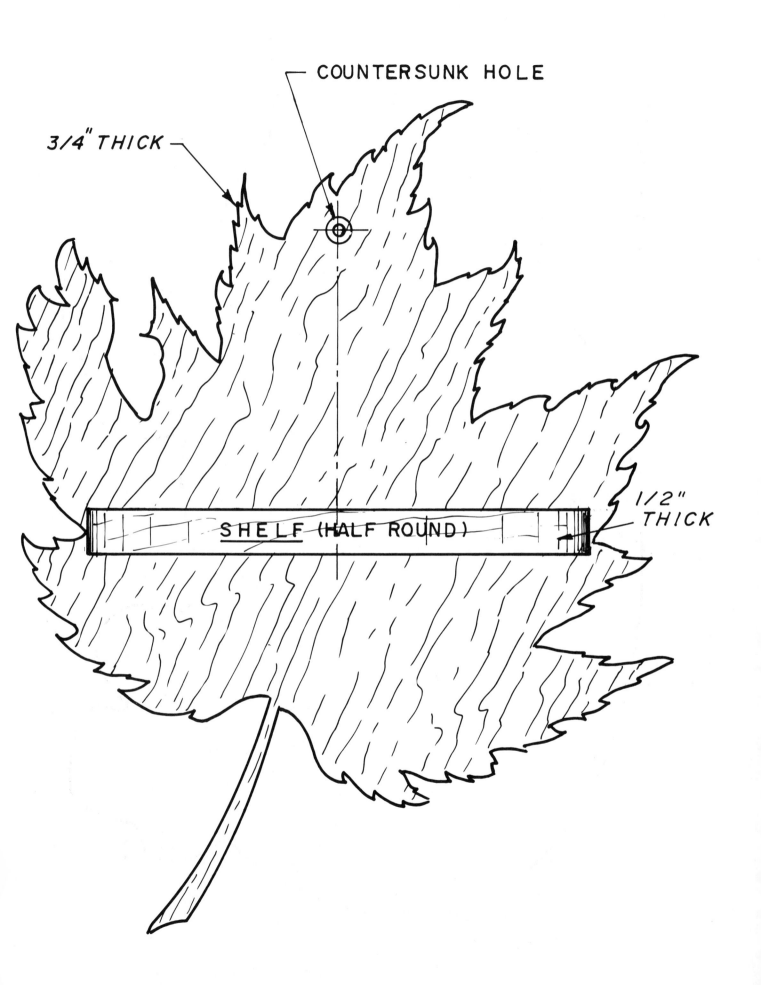

COUNTERSUNK HOLE

3/4" THICK

SHELF (HALF ROUND)

1/2" THICK

5/8" THICK

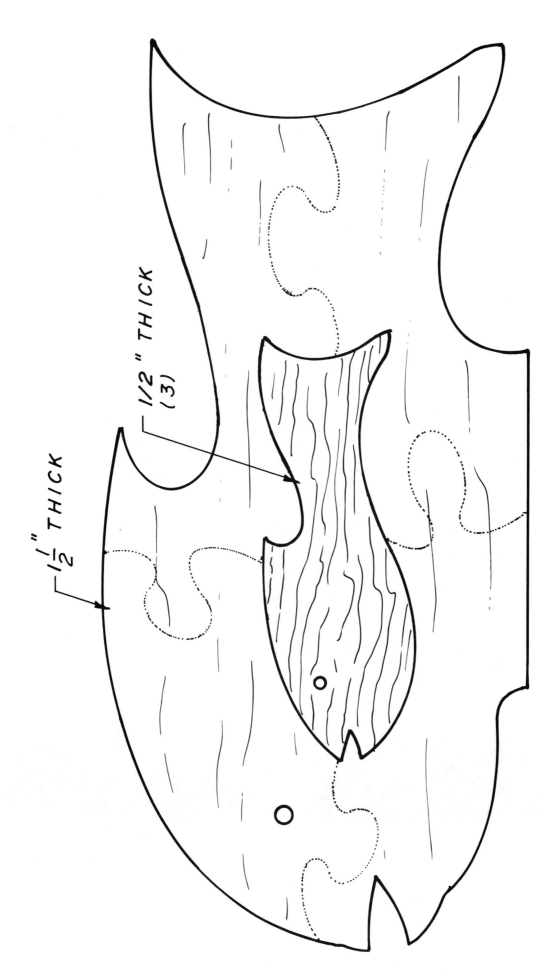

1/2" THICK
(3)

1½" THICK

1/2" TO 3/4" THICK

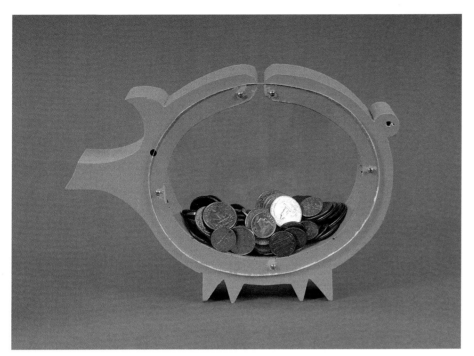

129

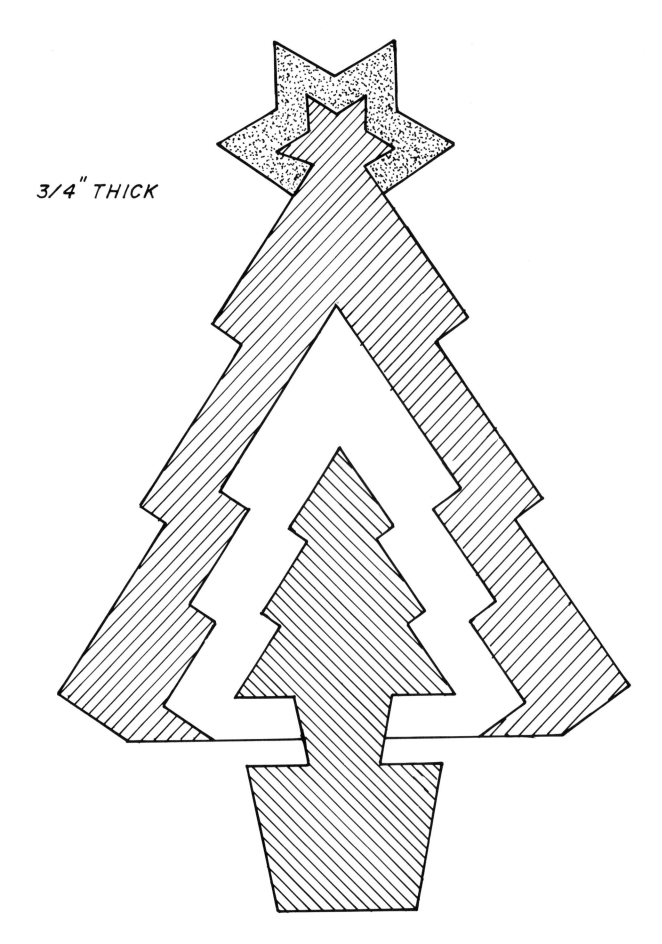

3/4" THICK

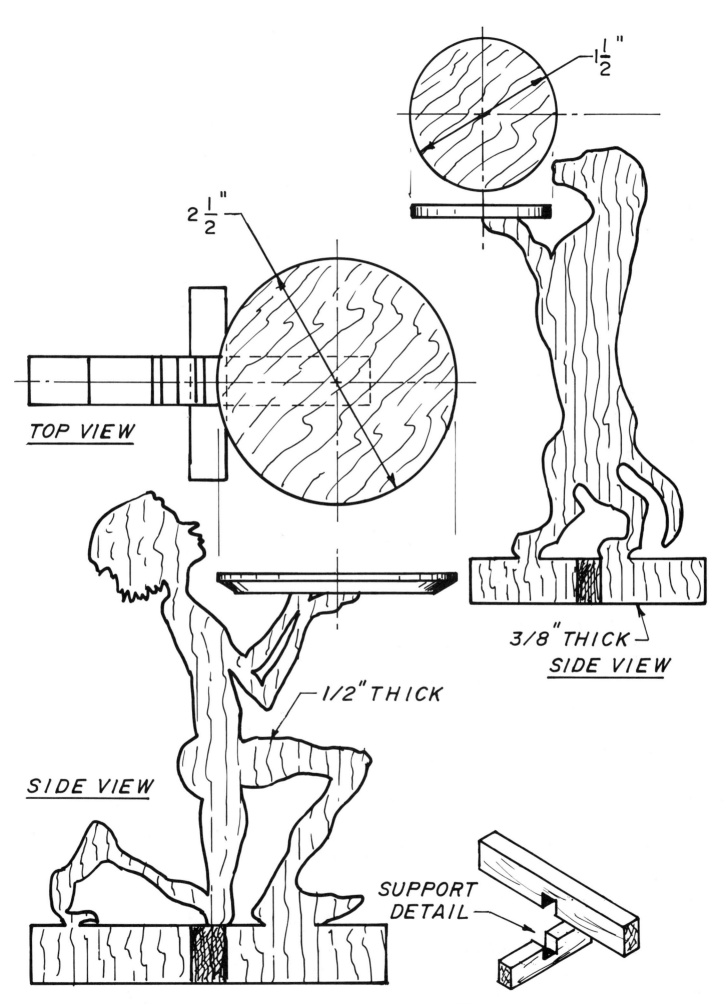

$2\frac{1}{2}$"

TOP VIEW

$1\frac{1}{2}$"

3/8" THICK
SIDE VIEW

1/2" THICK

SIDE VIEW

SUPPORT
DETAIL

131

MEISEL HARDWARE
NO. 6300 (3/4") OR EQUIVALENT

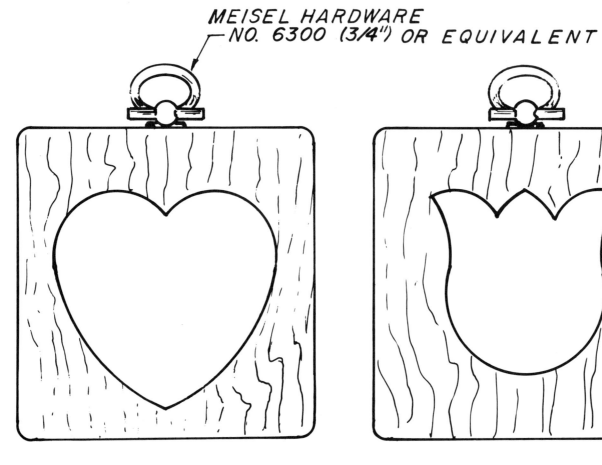

132

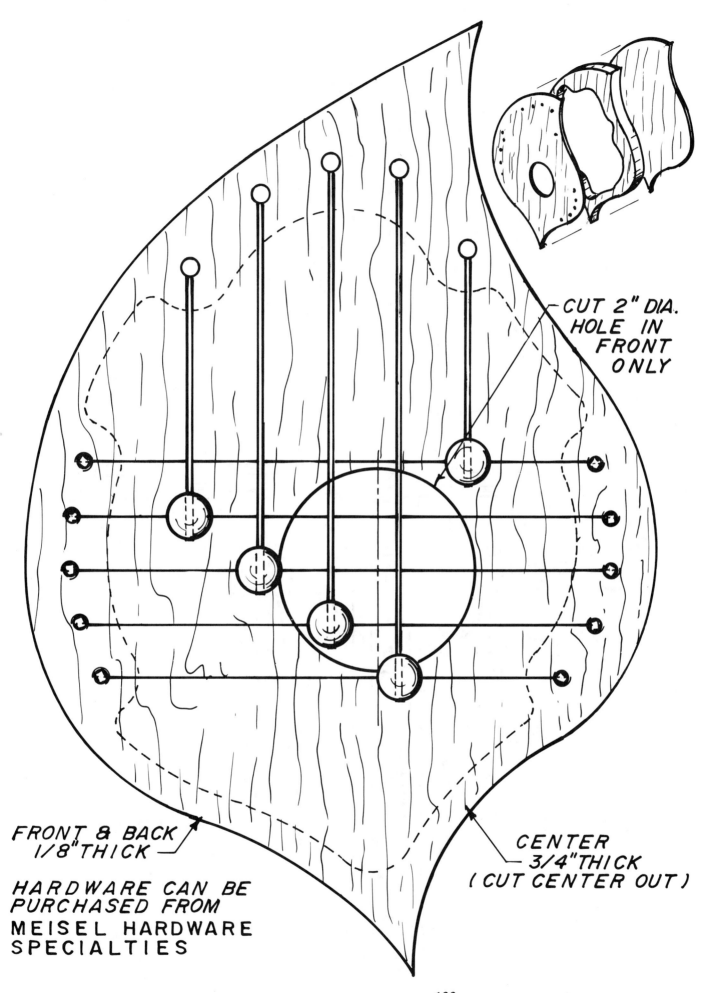

CUT 2" DIA. HOLE IN FRONT ONLY

FRONT & BACK 1/8"THICK

HARDWARE CAN BE PURCHASED FROM MEISEL HARDWARE SPECIALTIES

CENTER 3/4"THICK (CUT CENTER OUT)

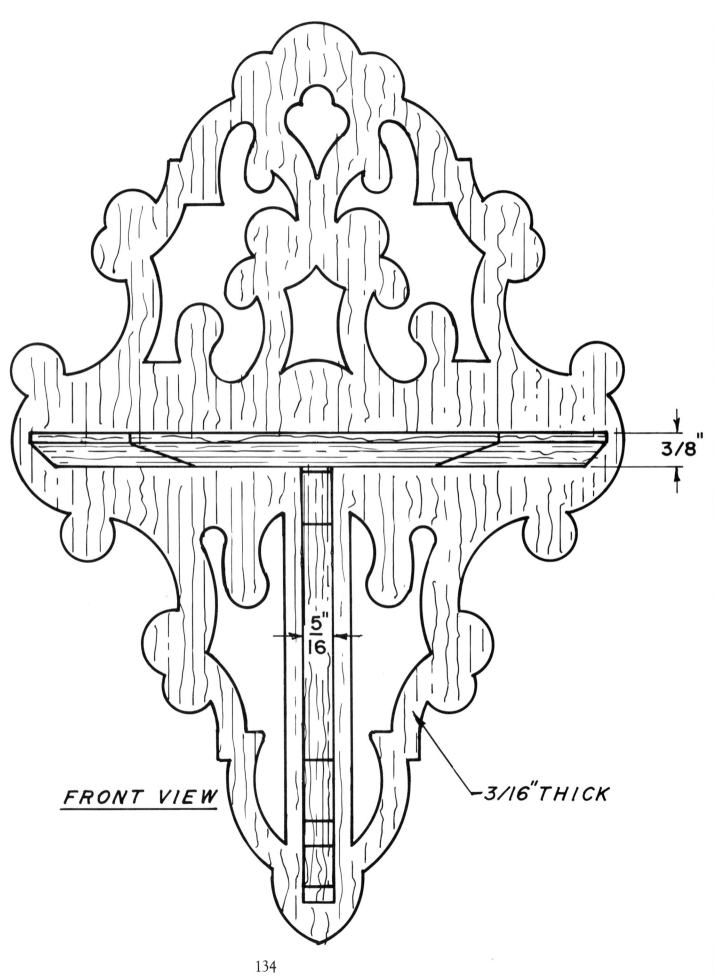

3/8"

$\frac{5"}{16}$

FRONT VIEW

—3/16" THICK

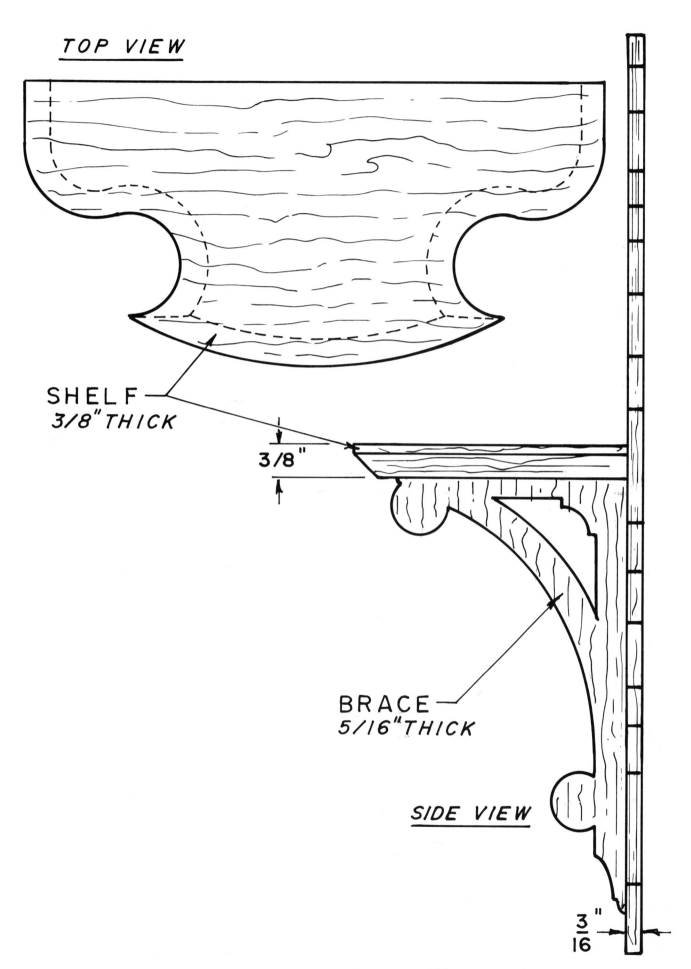

TOP VIEW

SHELF
3/8" THICK

3/8"

BRACE
5/16" THICK

SIDE VIEW

3/16"

135

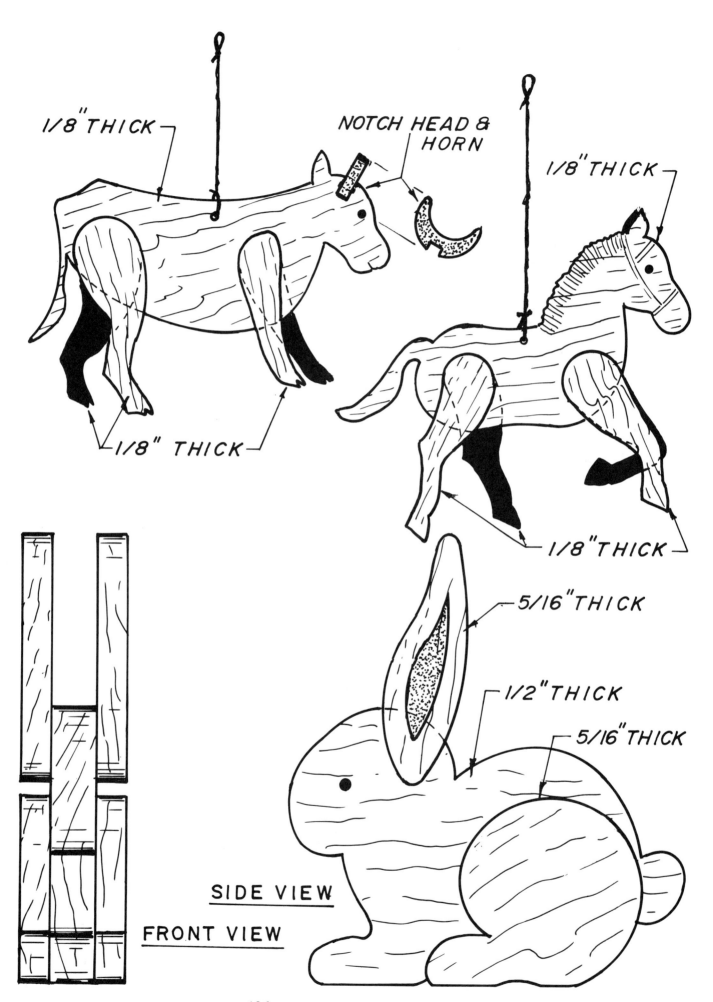

1/8" THICK

NOTCH HEAD & HORN

1/8" THICK

1/8" THICK

1/8" THICK

5/16" THICK

1/2" THICK

5/16" THICK

SIDE VIEW

FRONT VIEW

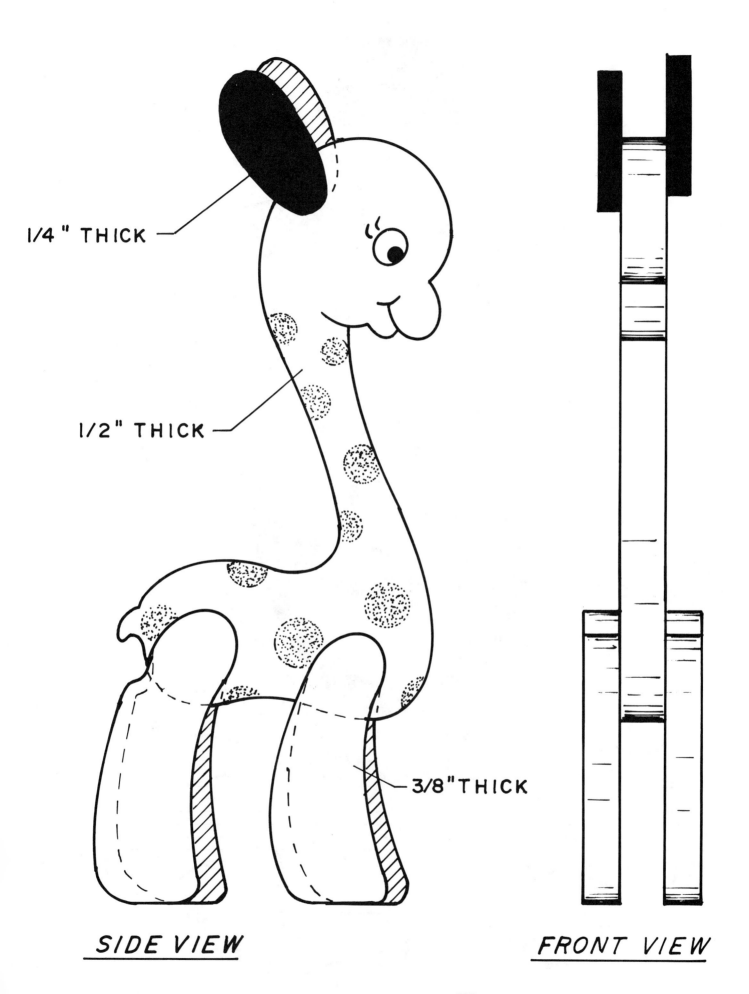

1/4 " THICK

1/2" THICK

3/8"THICK

SIDE VIEW

FRONT VIEW

137

3/4" THICK

TOUCH 'N' PLAY
MUSIC BOX
NO, 7855 OR
7856 FROM
MEISEL HARDWARE

1 3/16" HOLE
3/8" DEEP

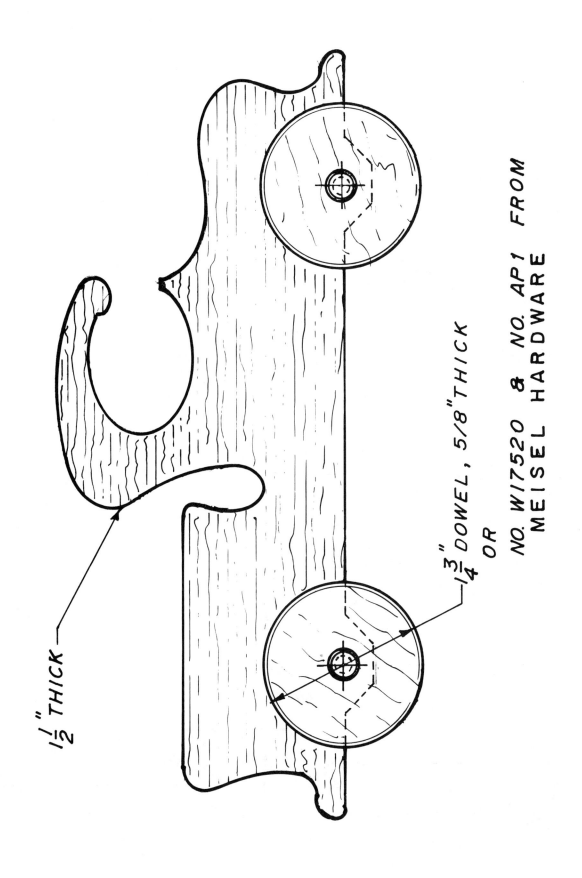

$1\frac{1}{2}''$ THICK

$1\frac{3}{4}''$ DOWEL, 5/8" THICK
OR

NO. W17520 & NO. AP1 FROM
MEISEL HARDWARE

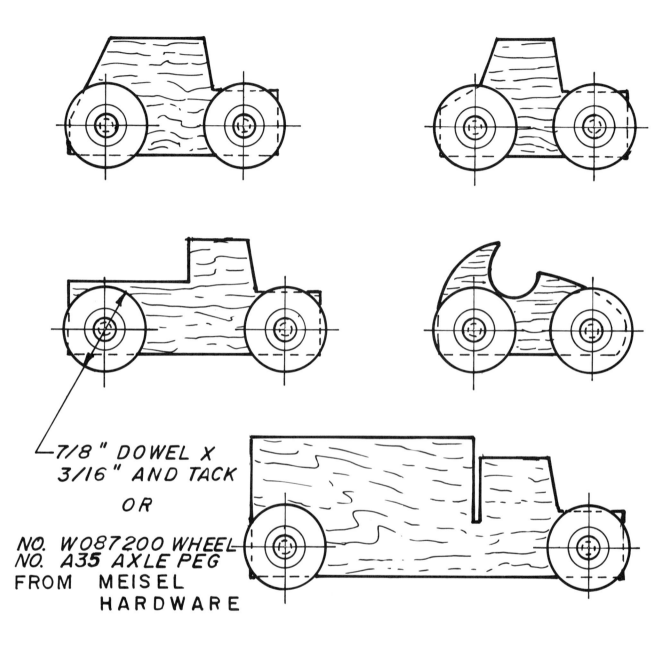

7/8" DOWEL X
3/16" AND TACK

OR

NO. W087200 WHEEL
NO. A35 AXLE PEG
FROM MEISEL
HARDWARE

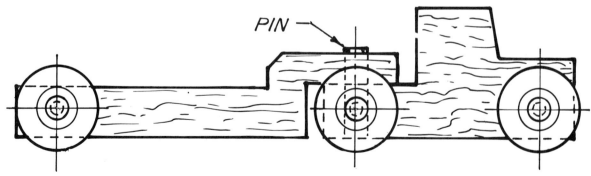

PIN

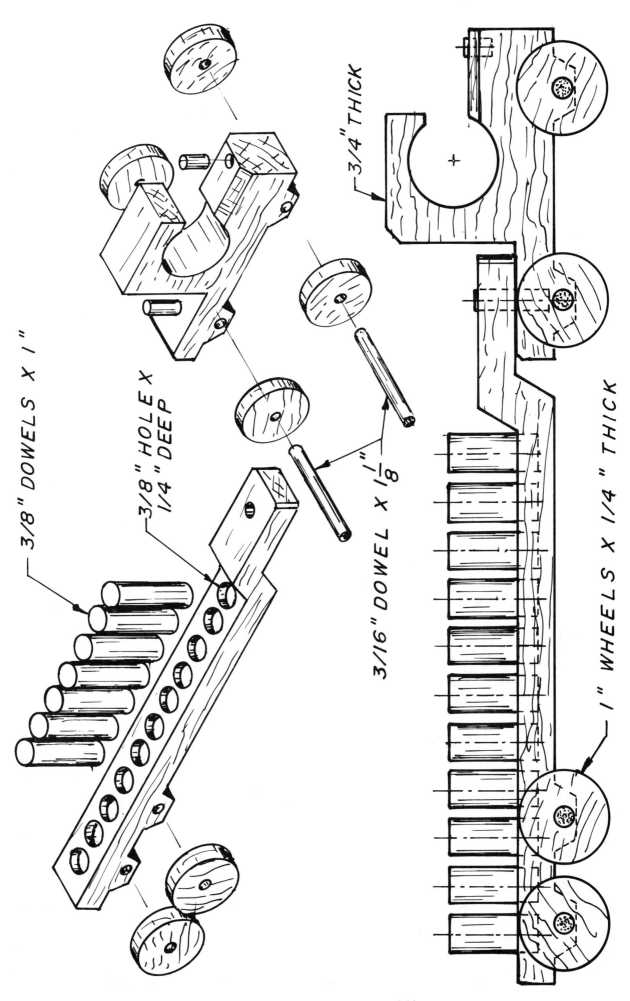

3/8" DOWELS X 1"

3/8" HOLE X 1/4" DEEP

3/16" DOWEL X 1⅛"

3/4" THICK

1" WHEELS X 1/4" THICK

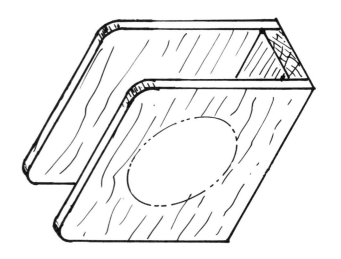

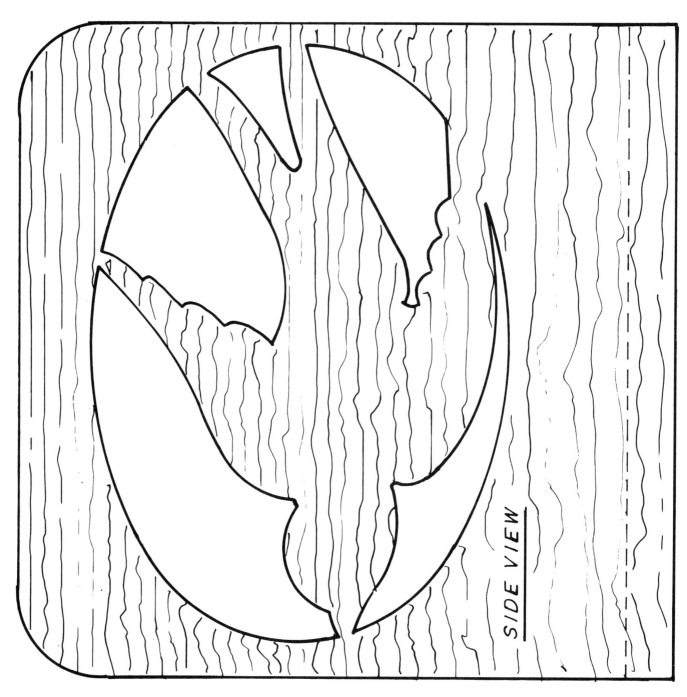

SIDE VIEW

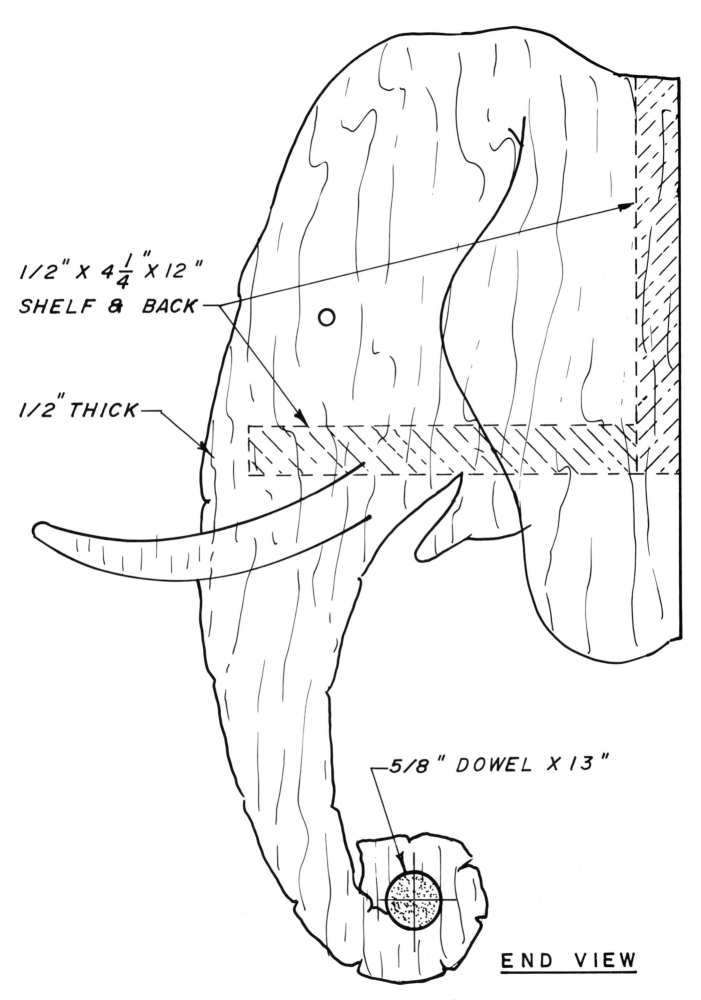

1/2" X 4$\frac{1}{4}$" X 12" SHELF & BACK

1/2" THICK

5/8" DOWEL X 13"

END VIEW

143

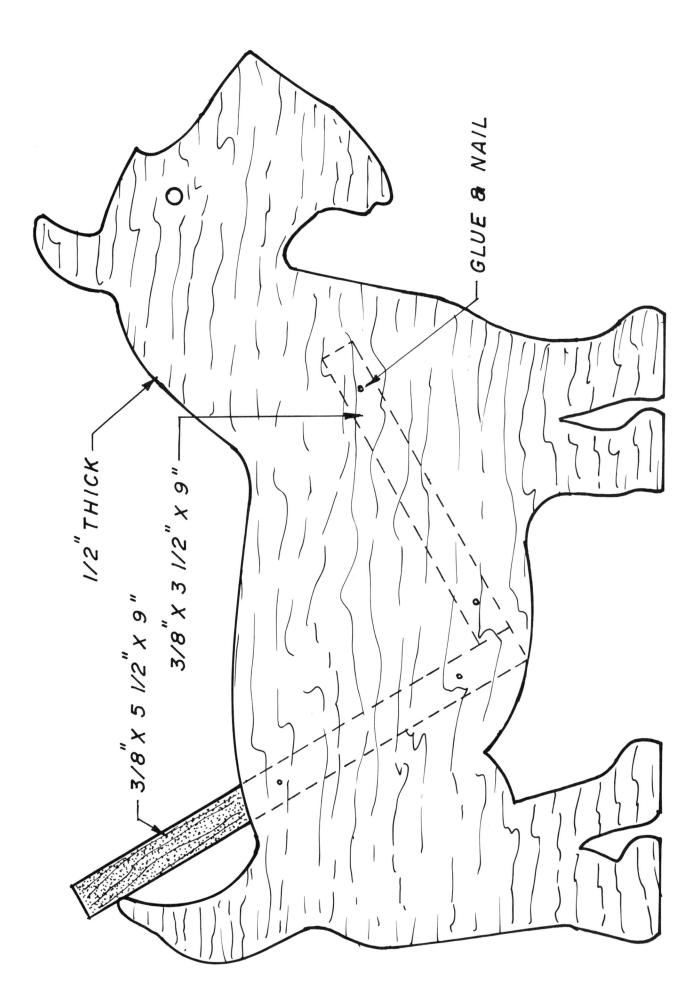

GLUE & NAIL

1/2" THICK

3/8" X 5 1/2" X 9"

3/8" X 3 1/2" X 9"

ENDS (2)
1/4" THICK

BACK
5/16" X 5 1/2" X 12"

BASE
5/16" X 4 1/4" X 12"

GLUE & NAIL BACK & BRACE TO ENDS

145

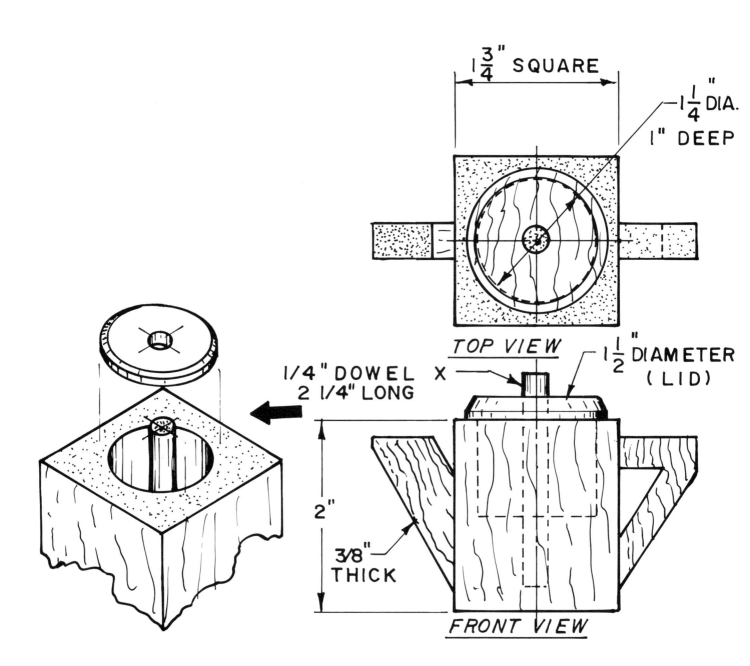

$1\frac{3}{4}"$ SQUARE

$1\frac{1}{4}"$ DIA.
1" DEEP

TOP VIEW

1/4" DOWEL X
2 1/4" LONG

$1\frac{1}{2}"$ DIAMETER
(LID)

2"

3/8" THICK

FRONT VIEW

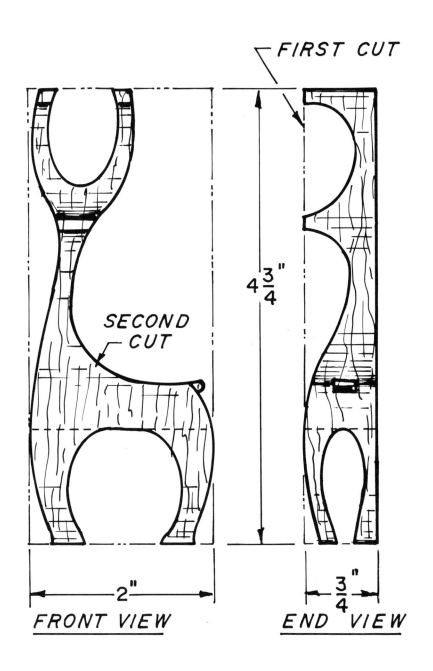

FIRST CUT

SECOND
CUT

$4\frac{3}{4}"$

$2"$

FRONT VIEW

$\frac{3}{4}"$

END VIEW

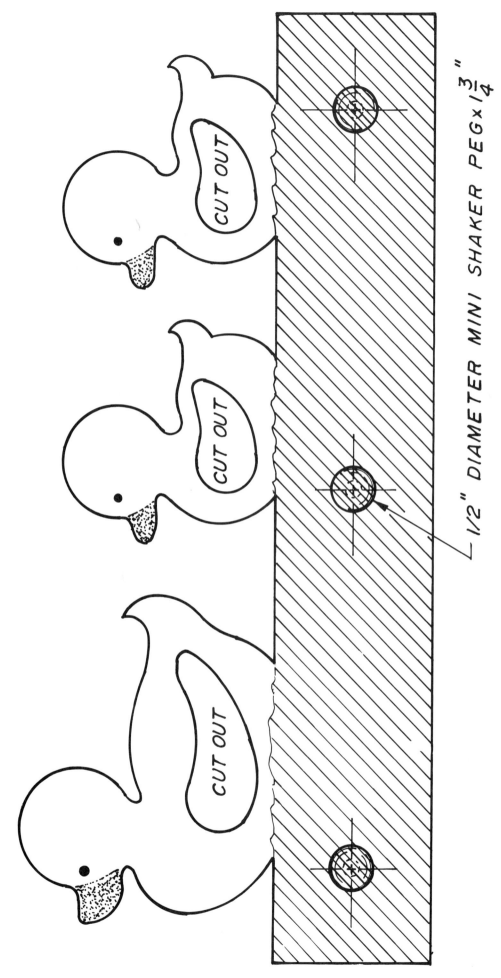

1/2" DIAMETER MINI SHAKER PEG×1¾"

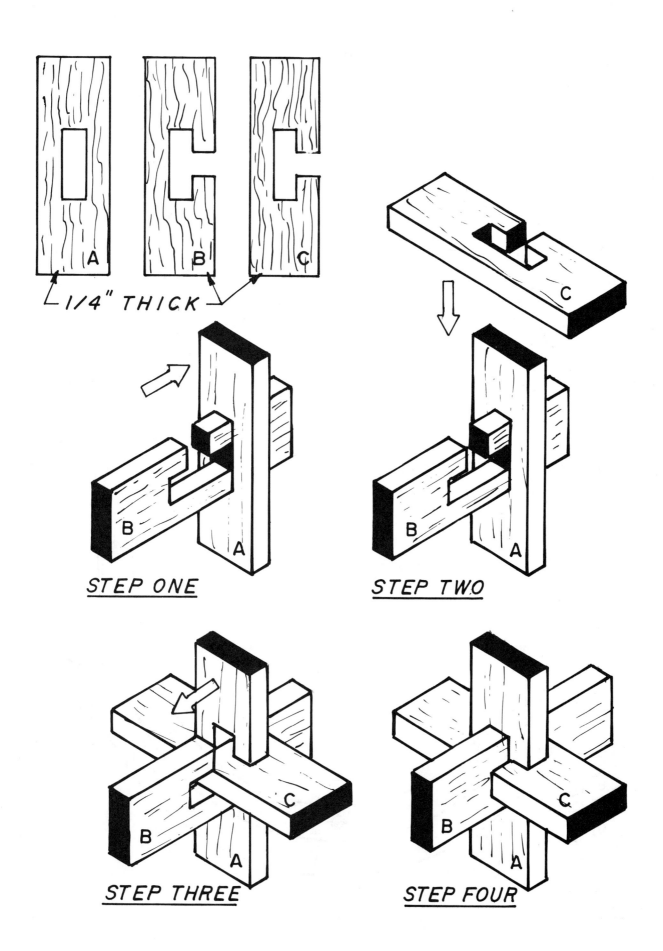

1/4" THICK

STEP ONE

STEP TWO

STEP THREE

STEP FOUR

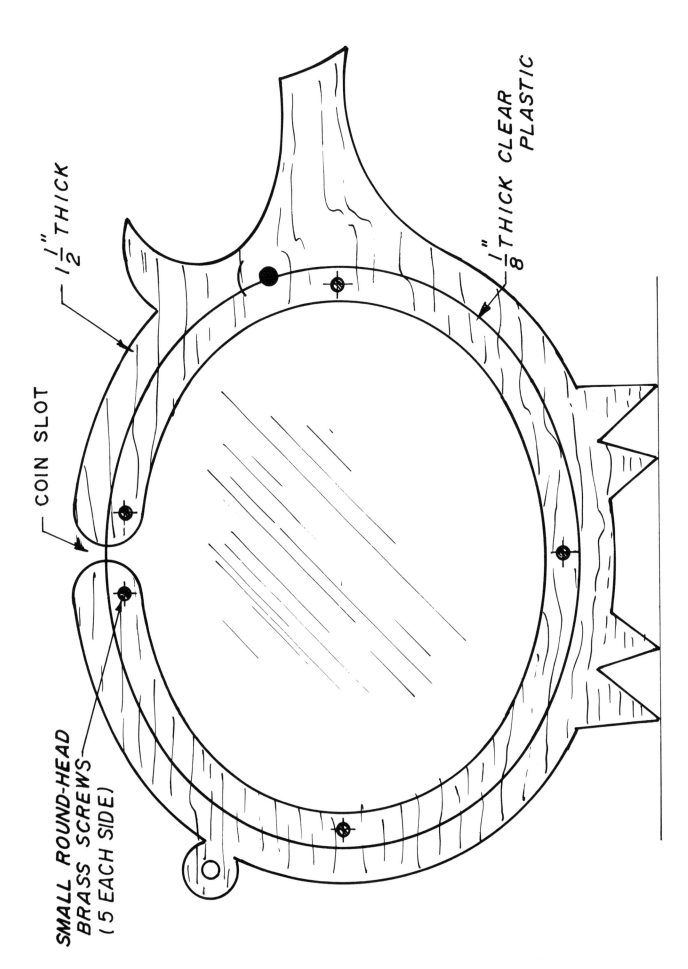

COIN SLOT

$1\frac{1}{2}$" THICK

SMALL ROUND-HEAD
BRASS SCREWS
(5 EACH SIDE)

$\frac{1}{8}$" THICK CLEAR
PLASTIC

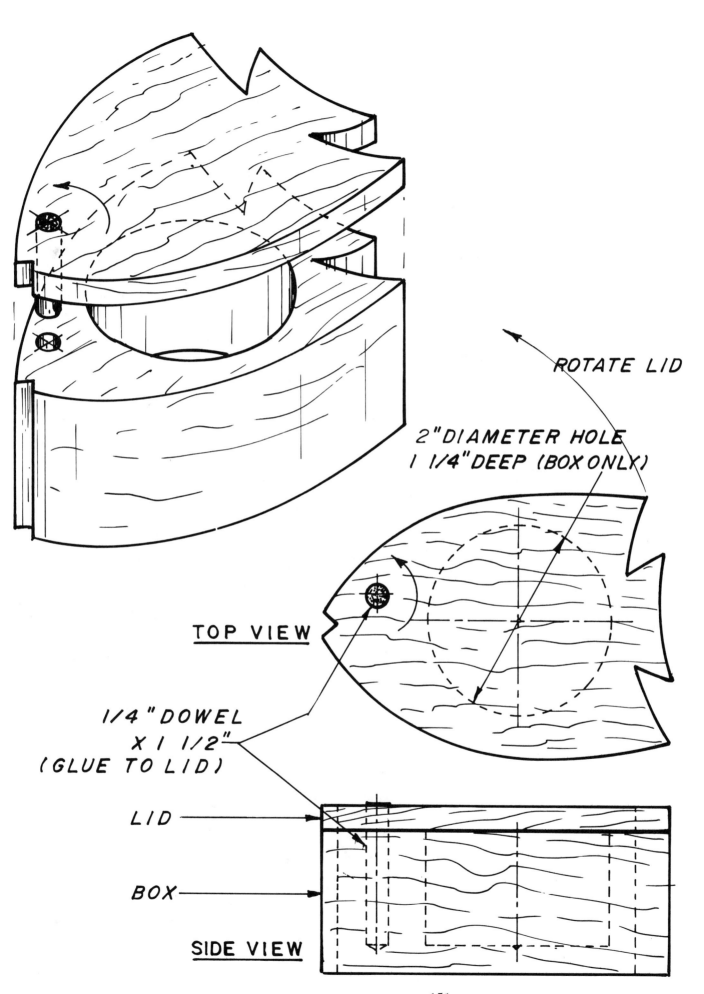

ROTATE LID

2" DIAMETER HOLE
1 1/4" DEEP (BOX ONLY)

TOP VIEW

1/4" DOWEL
X 1 1/2"
(GLUE TO LID)

LID

BOX

SIDE VIEW

151

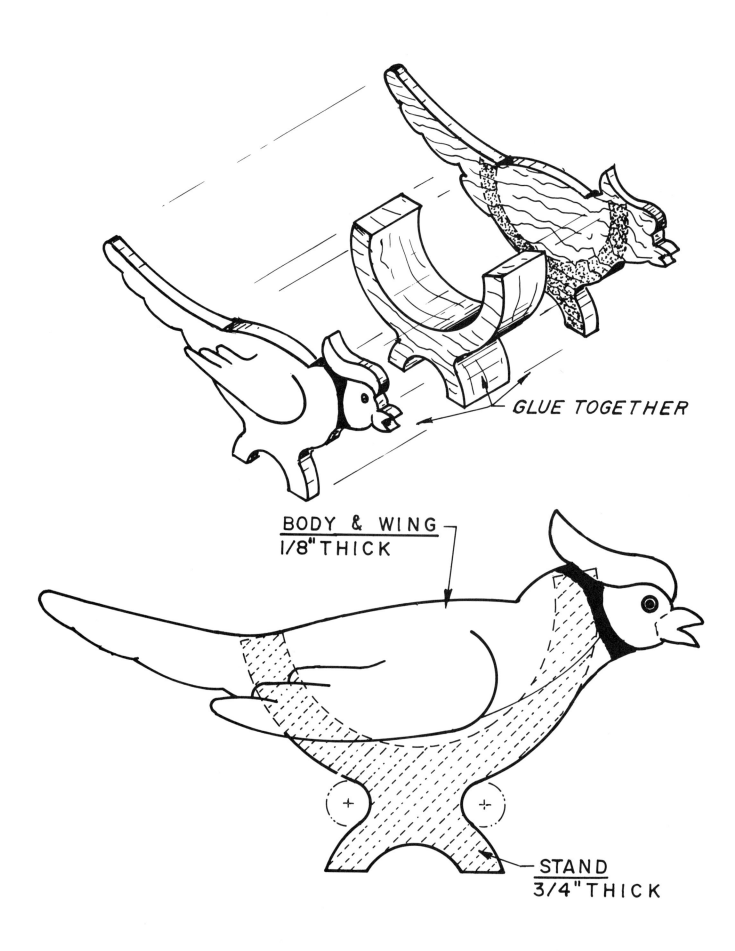

GLUE TOGETHER

BODY & WING
1/8"THICK

STAND
3/4"THICK

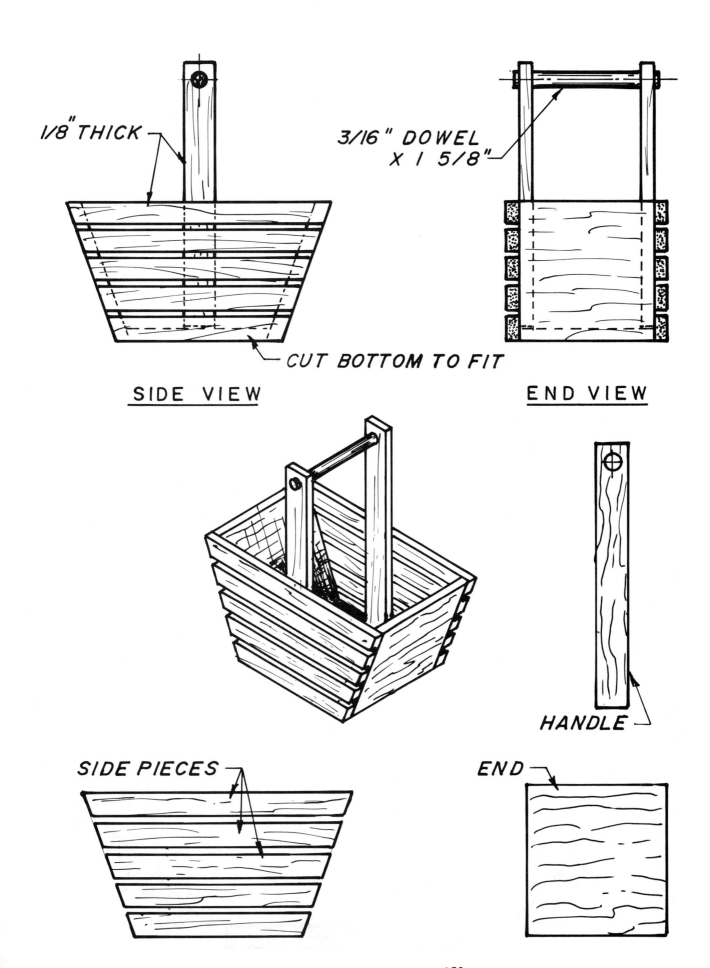

1/8" THICK

3/16" DOWEL
X 1 5/8"

CUT BOTTOM TO FIT

SIDE VIEW

END VIEW

HANDLE

SIDE PIECES

END

153

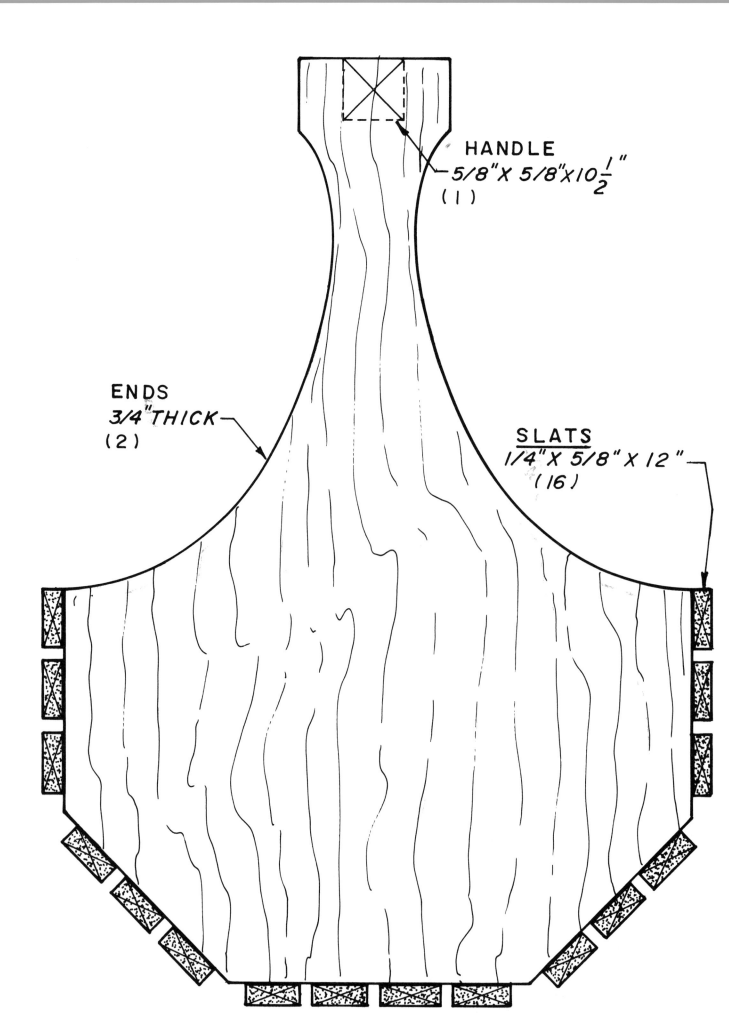

HANDLE
5/8" X 5/8" X 10$\frac{1}{2}$"
(1)

ENDS
3/4" THICK
(2)

SLATS
1/4" X 5/8" X 12"
(16)

154

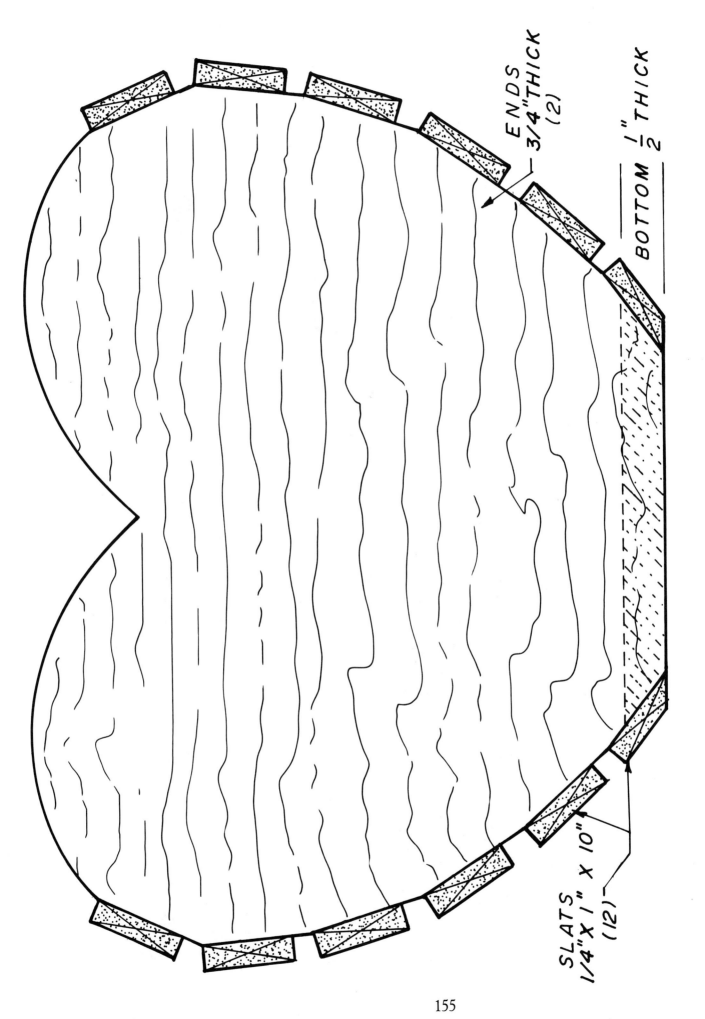

ENDS
3/4" THICK
(2)

BOTTOM $\frac{1}{2}$" THICK

SLATS
1/4" X 1" X 10"
(12)

$1\frac{1}{2}"$ THICK

FIT-UP MOVEMENT
KLOCKIT NO. 15002
OR EQUIVALENT

FIT-UP MOVEMENT
KLOCKIT NO. 15002
OR EQUIVALENT

$1\frac{1}{2}''$ THICK

FIT-UP MOVEMENT
KLOCKIT NO. 15002 OR EQUIVALENT

$1\frac{1}{2}"$ THICK

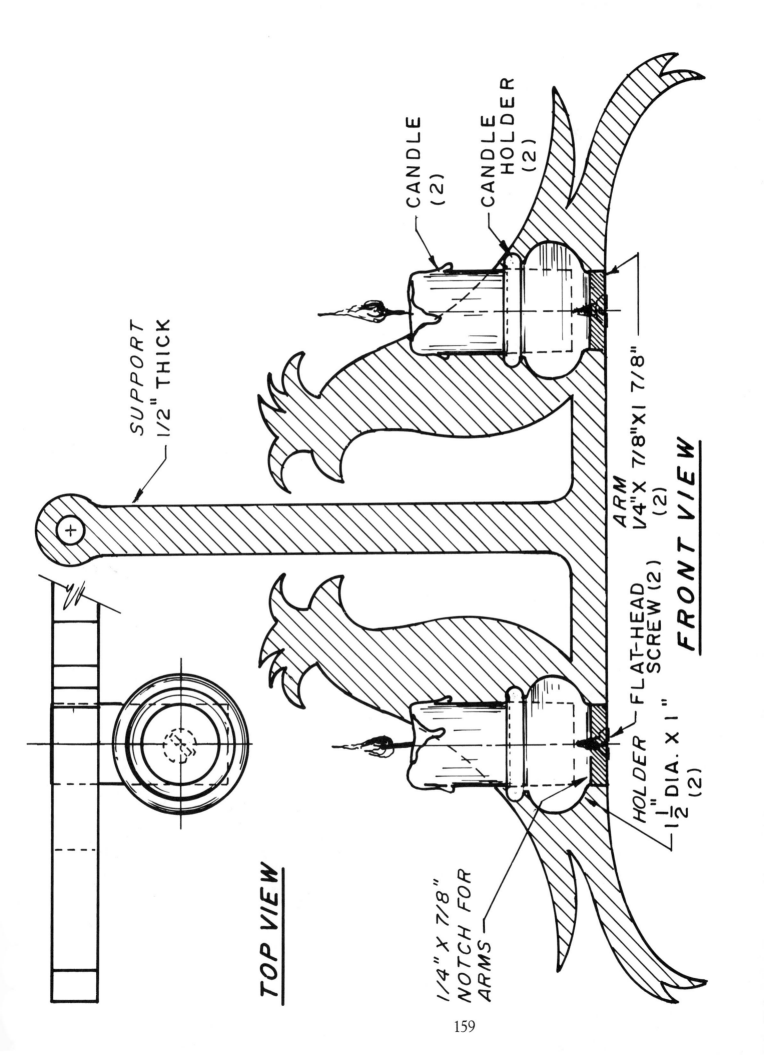

CANDLE (2)

CANDLE HOLDER (2)

SUPPORT 1/2" THICK

ARM 1/4" X 7/8" X 1 7/8" (2)

FRONT VIEW

HOLDER FLAT-HEAD SCREW (2)
1½" DIA. X 1" (2)

1/4" X 7/8" NOTCH FOR ARMS

TOP VIEW

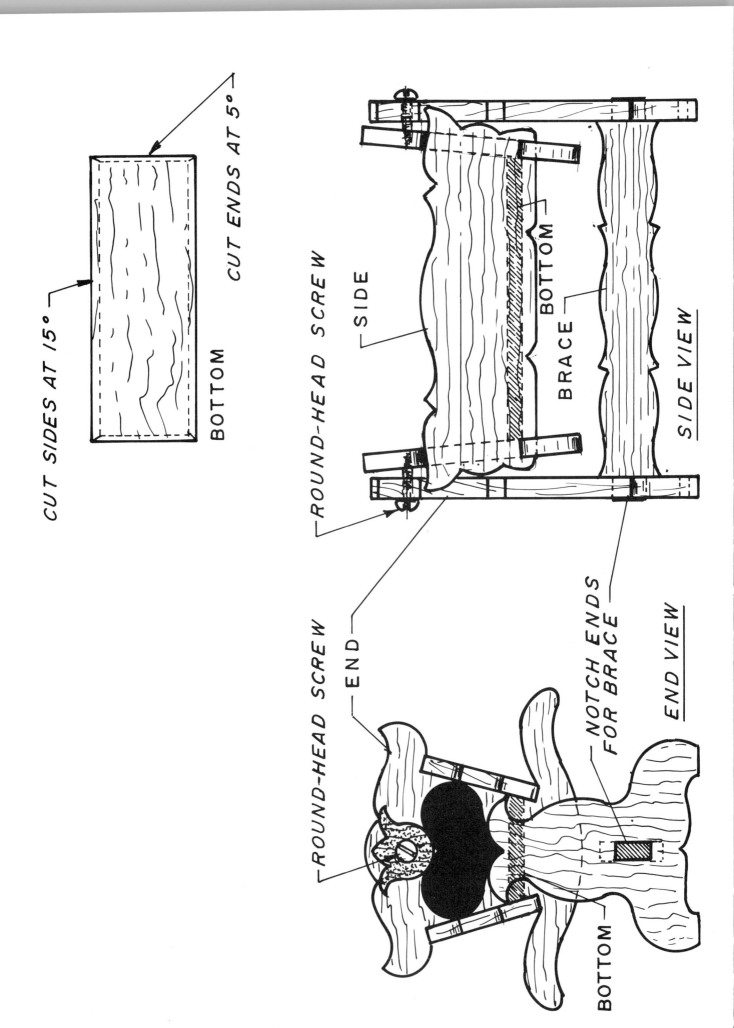

CUT SIDES AT 15°

CUT ENDS AT 5°

BOTTOM

ROUND-HEAD SCREW

SIDE

BRACE

BOTTOM

SIDE VIEW

ROUND-HEAD SCREW

END

NOTCH ENDS FOR BRACE

END VIEW

BOTTOM

STAND (2)

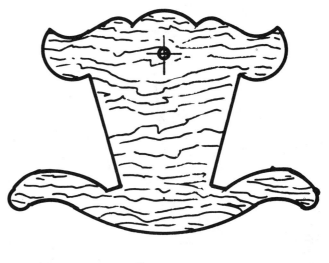

END (2)

BRACE (1)

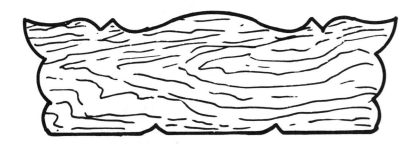

SIDE (2)

Use glue to attach the sides and ends to the bottom.

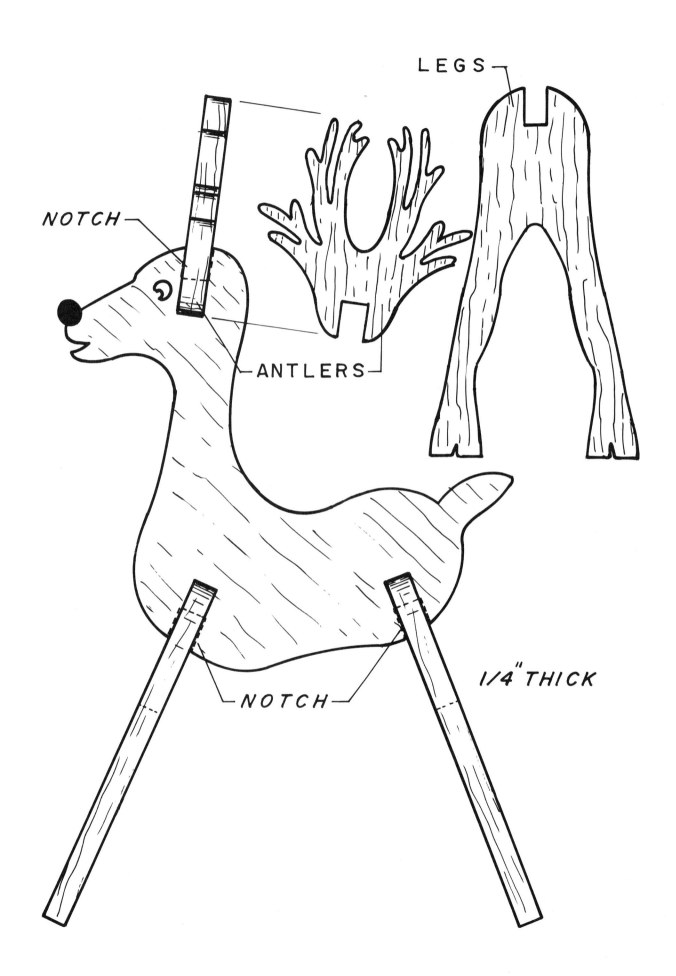

LEGS

NOTCH

ANTLERS

NOTCH

1/4" THICK

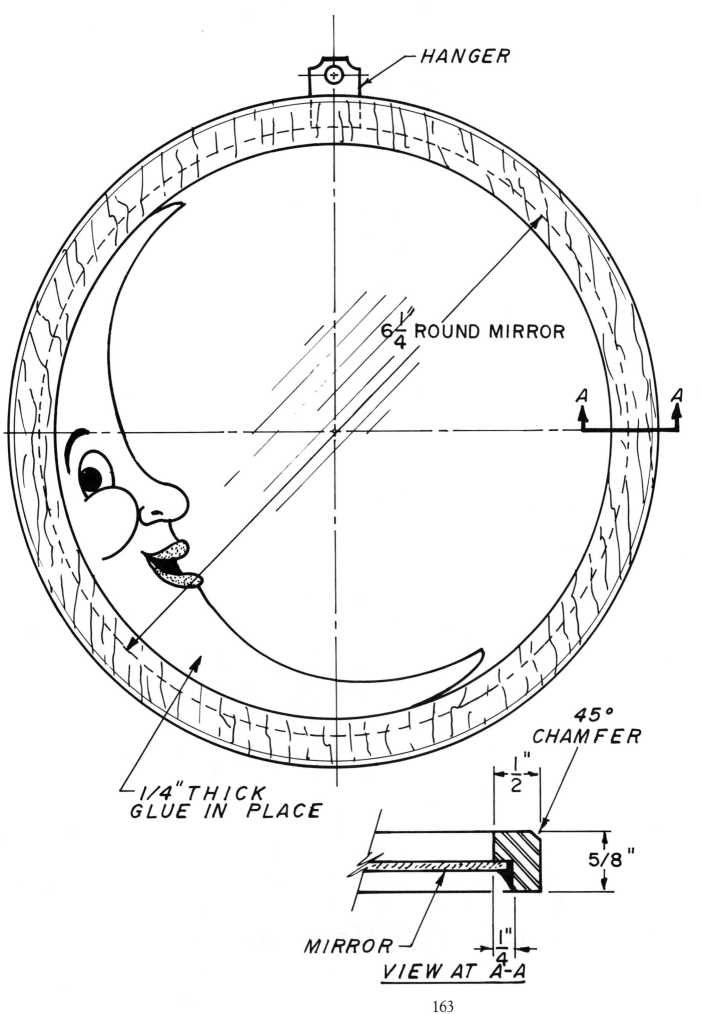

HANGER

$6\frac{1}{4}$ ROUND MIRROR

A   A

1/4" THICK
GLUE IN PLACE

45°
CHAMFER

$\frac{1}{2}$"

5/8"

MIRROR

$\frac{1}{4}$"

VIEW AT A-A

163

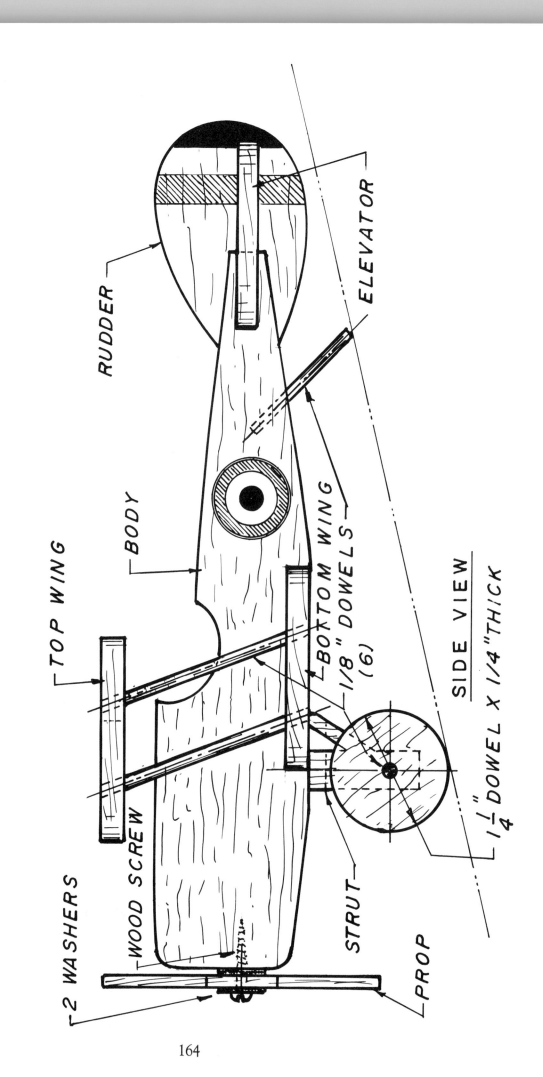

RUDDER

ELEVATOR

BODY

TOP WING

BOTTOM WING

1/8" DOWELS
(6)

SIDE VIEW

1¼" DOWEL X 1/4" THICK

WOOD SCREW

STRUT

2 WASHERS

PROP

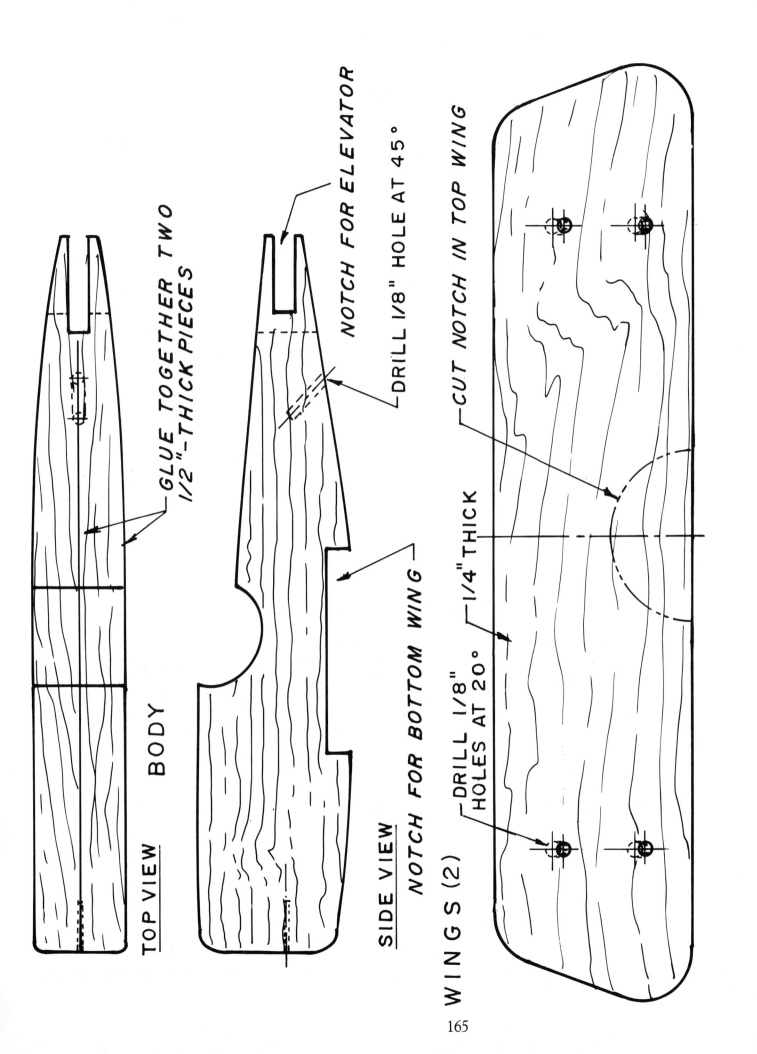

GLUE TOGETHER TWO 1/2"-THICK PIECES

TOP VIEW   BODY

NOTCH FOR ELEVATOR

DRILL 1/8" HOLE AT 45°

SIDE VIEW
NOTCH FOR BOTTOM WING

CUT NOTCH IN TOP WING

1/4" THICK

DRILL 1/8" HOLES AT 20°

W I N G S (2)

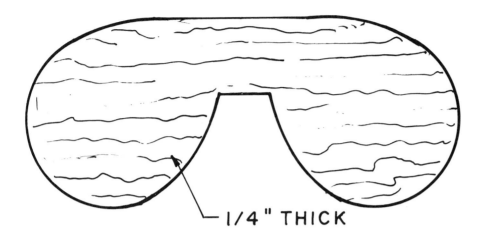

ELEVATOR

1/4" THICK

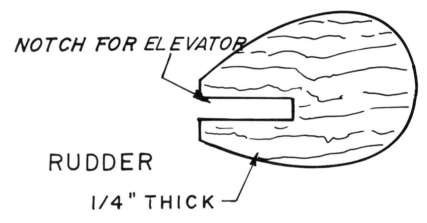

NOTCH FOR ELEVATOR

RUDDER

1/4" THICK

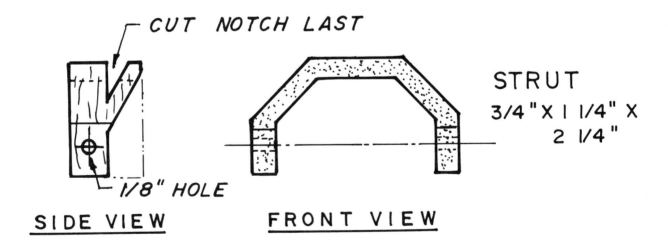

CUT NOTCH LAST

1/8" HOLE

SIDE VIEW

FRONT VIEW

STRUT
3/4" X 1 1/4" X
2 1/4"

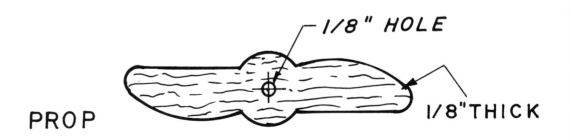

1/8" HOLE

1/8" THICK

PROP

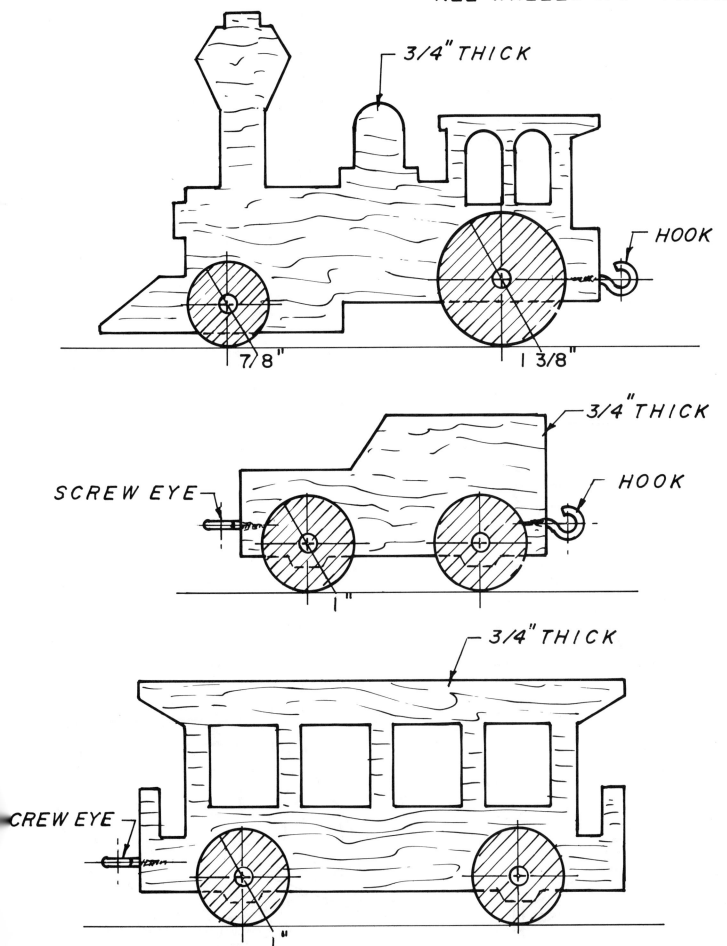

ALL WHEELS 3/8 " THICK

3/4" THICK

HOOK

7 8 "

1 3/8 "

3/4" THICK

SCREW EYE

HOOK

1 "

3/4" THICK

CREW EYE

1 "

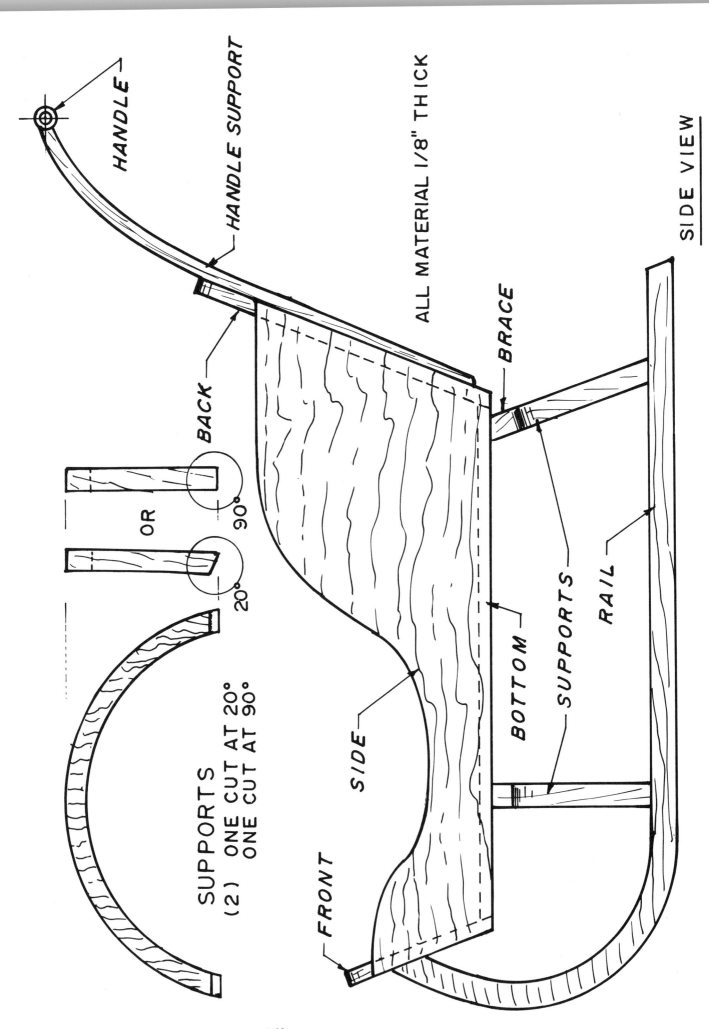

HANDLE

HANDLE SUPPORT

BACK

OR

90°

20°

SUPPORTS
(2) ONE CUT AT 20°
ONE CUT AT 90°

FRONT

SIDE

ALL MATERIAL 1/8" THICK

BRACE

BOTTOM

SUPPORTS

RAIL

SIDE VIEW

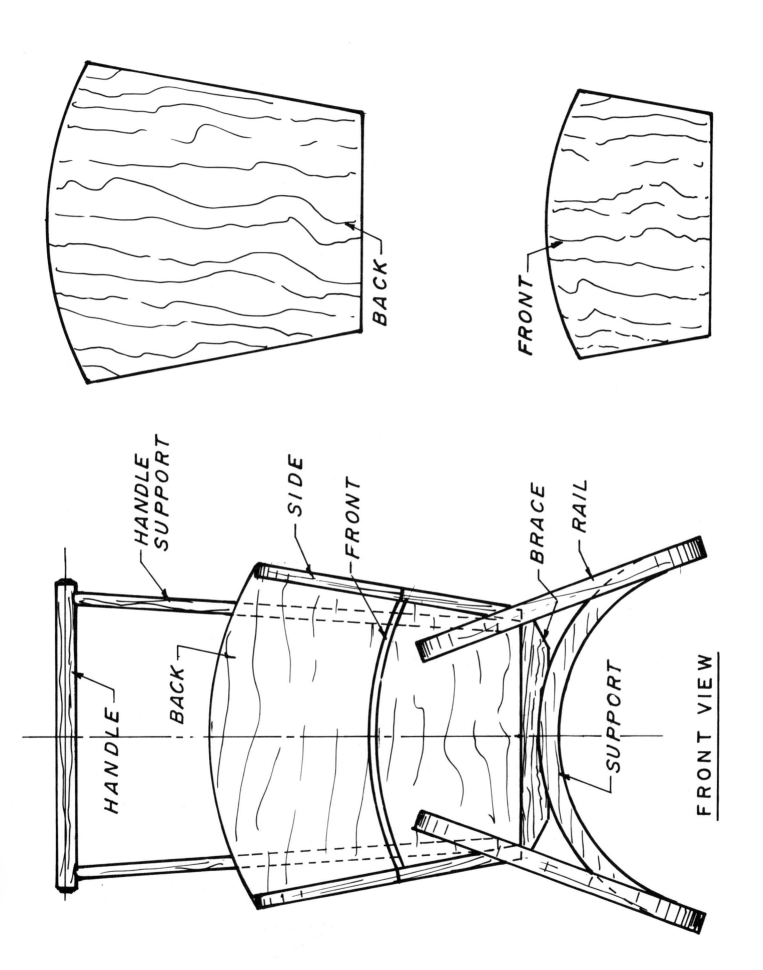

HANDLE SUPPORT

SIDE

FRONT

BRACE

RAIL

HANDLE

BACK

SUPPORT

FRONT VIEW

BACK

FRONT

FRONT

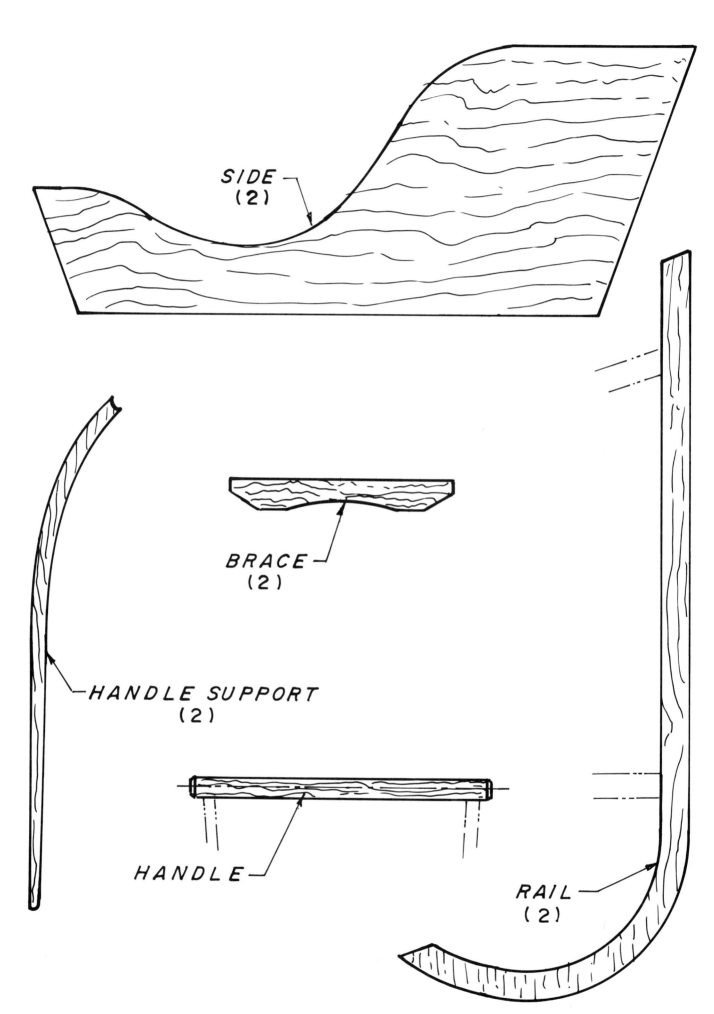

SIDE
(2)

BRACE
(2)

HANDLE SUPPORT
(2)

HANDLE

RAIL
(2)

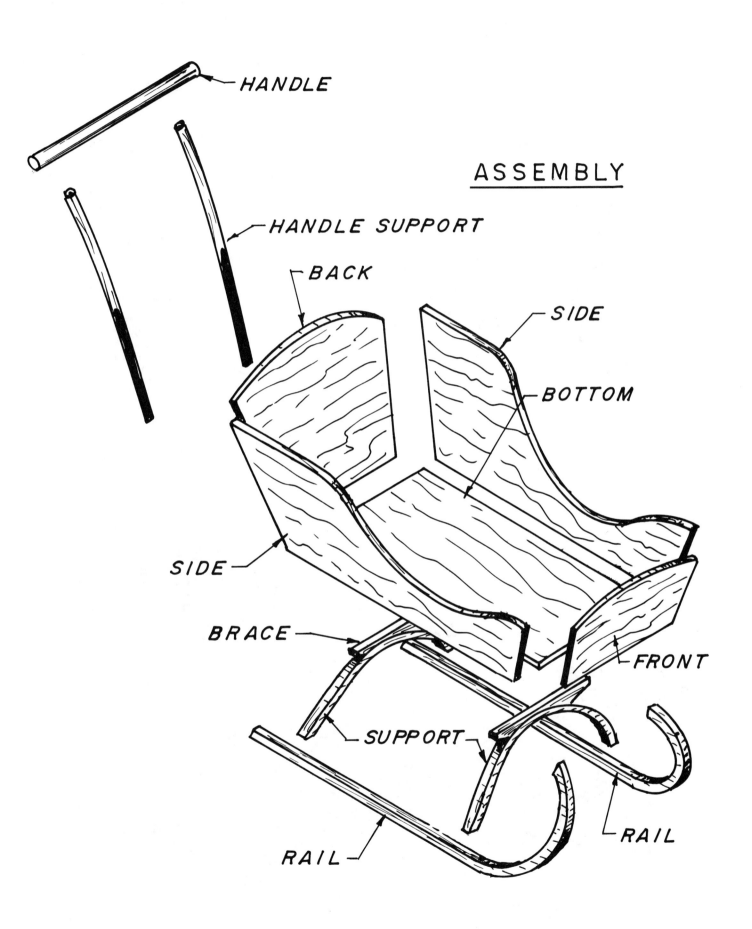

HANDLE

HANDLE SUPPORT

ASSEMBLY

BACK

SIDE

BOTTOM

SIDE

BRACE

SUPPORT

FRONT

RAIL

RAIL

171

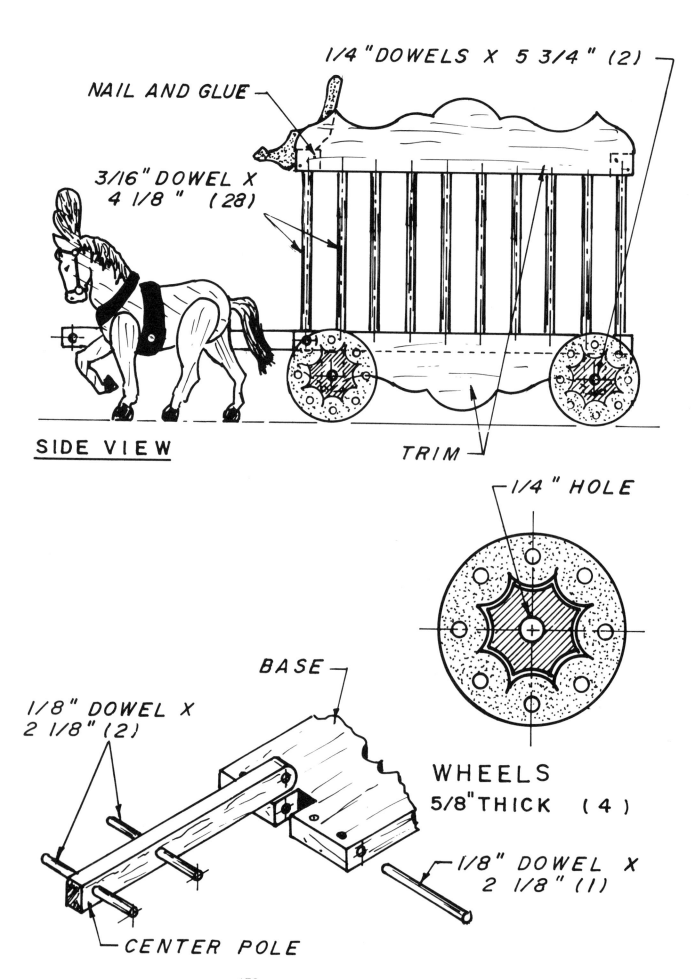

1/4" DOWELS X 5 3/4" (2)

NAIL AND GLUE

3/16" DOWEL X
4 1/8 " (28)

SIDE VIEW

TRIM

1/4 " HOLE

WHEELS
5/8" THICK (4)

1/8" DOWEL X
2 1/8" (2)

BASE

1/8" DOWEL X
2 1/8" (1)

CENTER POLE

172

TOP VIEW OF TRIM

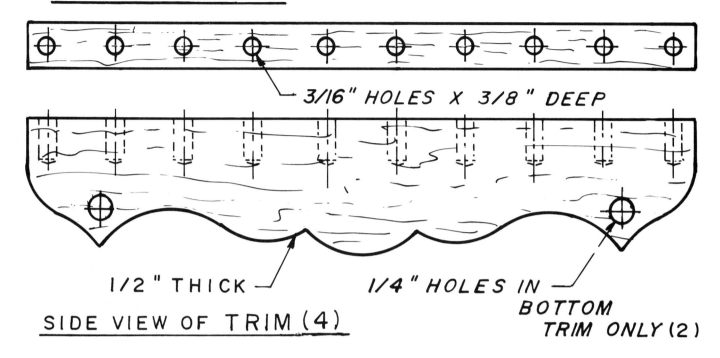

3/16" HOLES X 3/8" DEEP

1/2" THICK

1/4" HOLES IN BOTTOM TRIM ONLY (2)

SIDE VIEW OF TRIM (4)

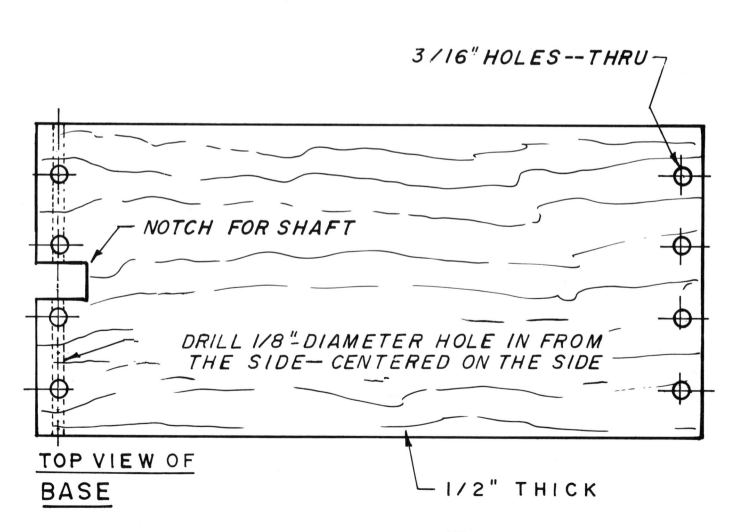

3/16" HOLES -- THRU

NOTCH FOR SHAFT

DRILL 1/8"-DIAMETER HOLE IN FROM THE SIDE — CENTERED ON THE SIDE

TOP VIEW OF BASE

1/2" THICK

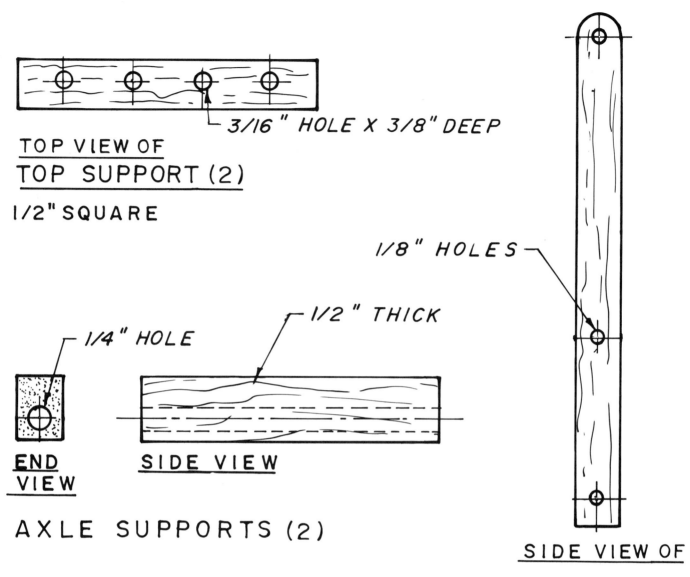

TOP VIEW OF
TOP SUPPORT (2)

1/2" SQUARE

3/16" HOLE X 3/8" DEEP

1/4" HOLE

1/2" THICK

END
VIEW

SIDE VIEW

AXLE SUPPORTS (2)

1/8" HOLES

SIDE VIEW OF

CENTER POLE
3/8" X 1/2" X 5 3/8"

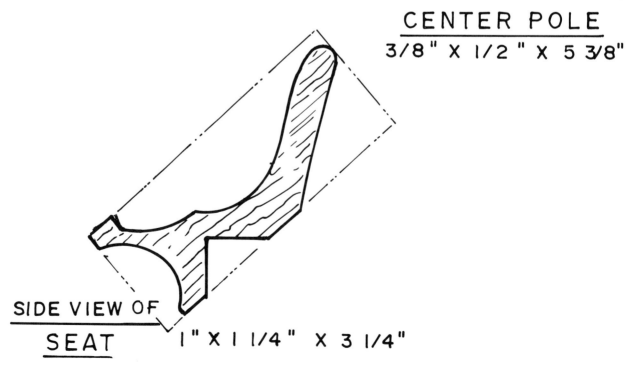

SIDE VIEW OF
SEAT

1" X 1 1/4" X 3 1/4"

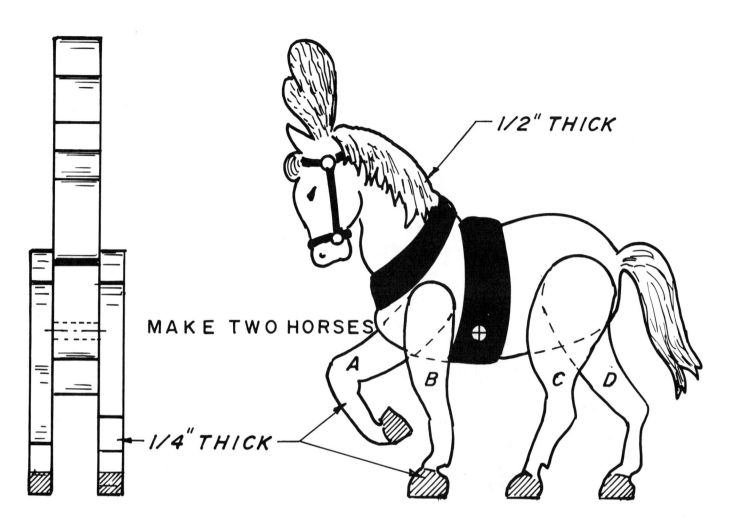

1/2" THICK

MAKE TWO HORSES

1/4" THICK

FRONT VIEW   SIDE VIEW

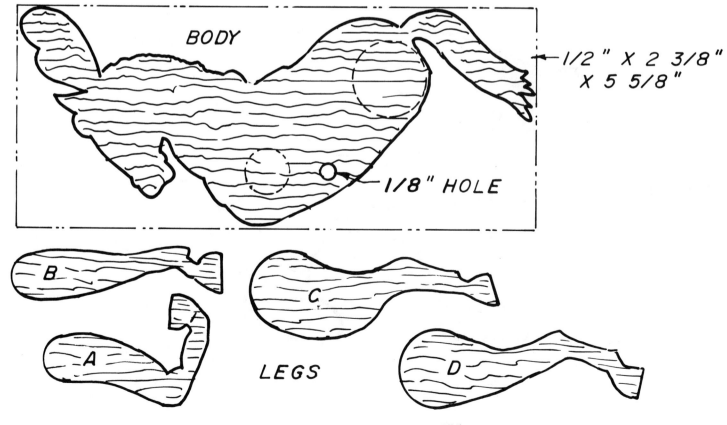

BODY

1/2" X 2 3/8" X 5 5/8"

1/8" HOLE

LEGS

B   A   C   D

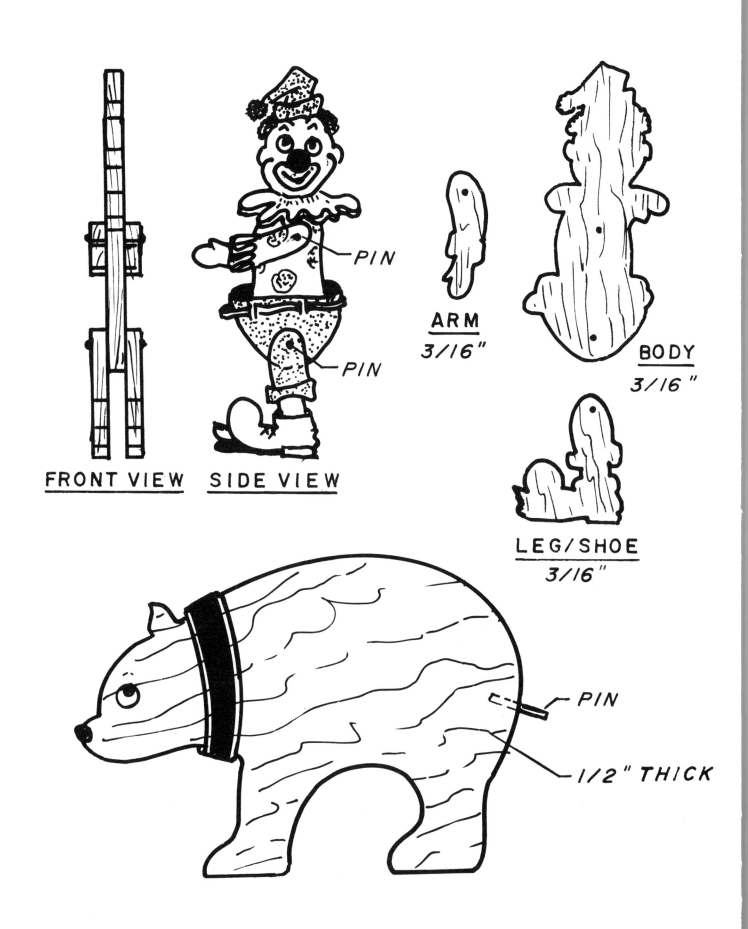

FRONT VIEW   SIDE VIEW

PIN

PIN

ARM
3/16"

BODY
3/16"

LEG/SHOE
3/16"

PIN

1/2" THICK

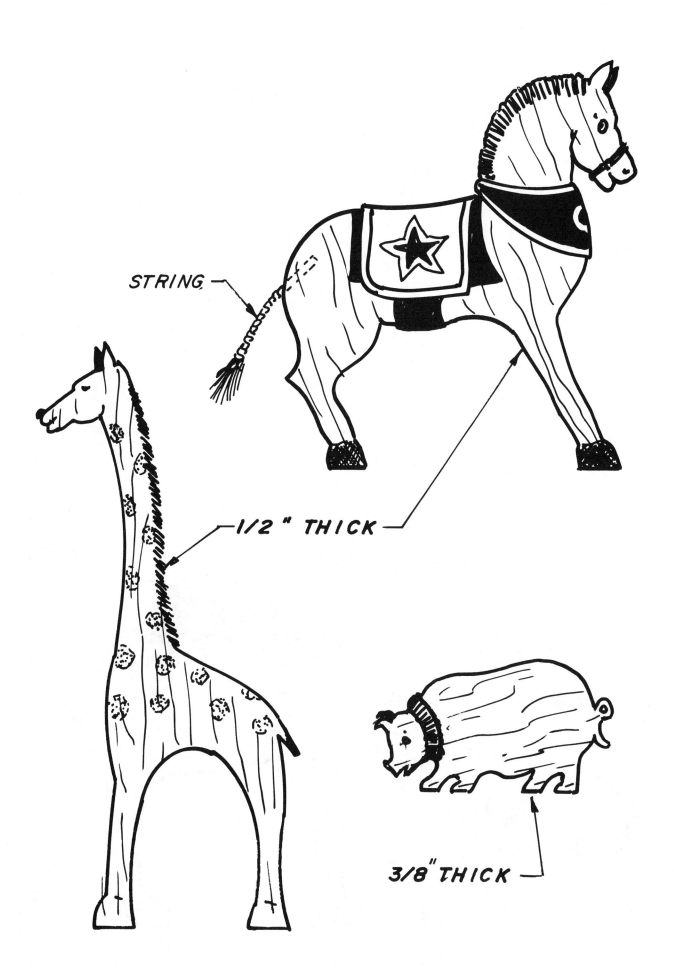

STRING

1/2" THICK

3/8" THICK

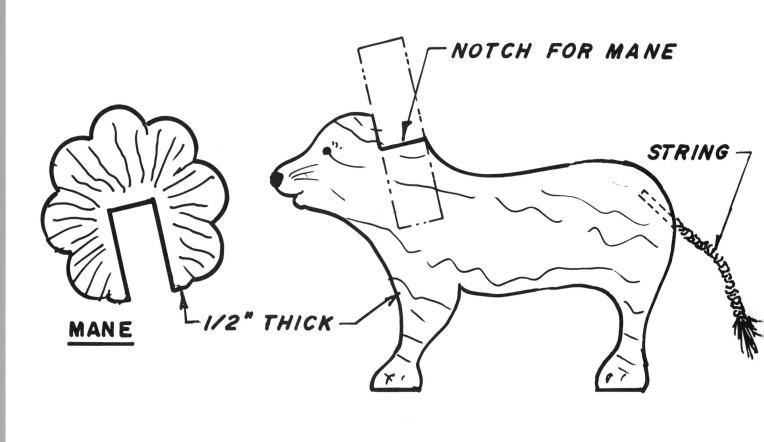

NOTCH FOR MANE

STRING

MANE

1/2" THICK

1/2" THICK

3/8" THICK

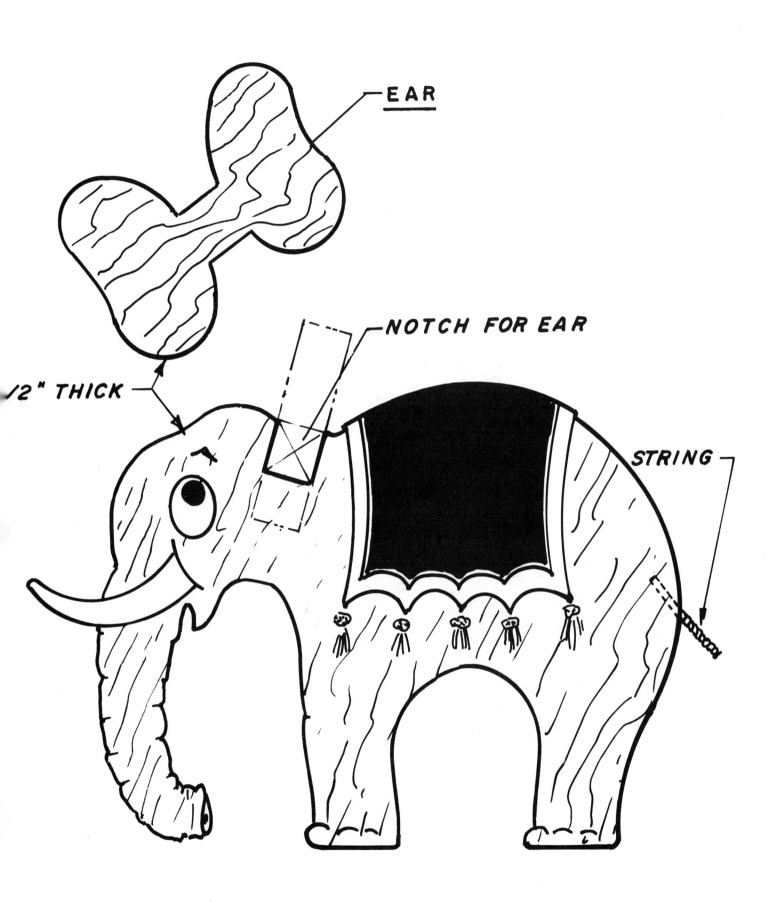

EAR

NOTCH FOR EAR

1/2" THICK

STRING

PIANO MUSIC BOX

NO.	NAME	SIZE	REQ'D.
1	BODY	1 3/8 X 6 – 7 7/8 LG.	1
2	BOTTOM	1/8 X 6 – 7 7/8 LG.	1
3	TOP	1/4 X 6 – 6 3/4 LONG	1
4	HINGE W/ SCREWS	NO. 125 OR EQUAL	3
5	SPACER	1/4 X 1/4 – 3/4 LONG	1
6	LID SUPPORT	1/8 DIA. – 3 1/4 LG.	1
7	SUPPORT	3/8 DIA. – 7/8 LONG	1
8	KEYBOARD	NO. 1648 OR EQUAL	1
9	KEYBOARD SPACER	3/16 X 5/16 – 15/16 LG.	2
10	FRONT BOARD	1/8 X 1/8 – 4 7/8 LONG	1
11	LEG SUPPORT	1/4 X 5/8 – 2 3/8 LG.	3
12	LEG TOP	3/8 X 1/2 – 1 3/4 LG.	3
13	LEG	1/2 X 1/2 – 2 1/8 LG.	3
14	LEG PIN	1/8 DIA. – 1 1/4 LG.	3
15	LYRE	1/2 X 1 1/2 – 2 3/4 LG.	1
16	PEDAL	1/8 DIA. – 5/8 LONG	3
17	MUSIC BOX	586 – K OR EQUAL	1
18	PAD (CORK)	3/8 DIA.	3

Parts 4, 8, and 17 can be purchased from Miesel Hardware
Specialties, P.O. Box 70, Mound, MN 55364.

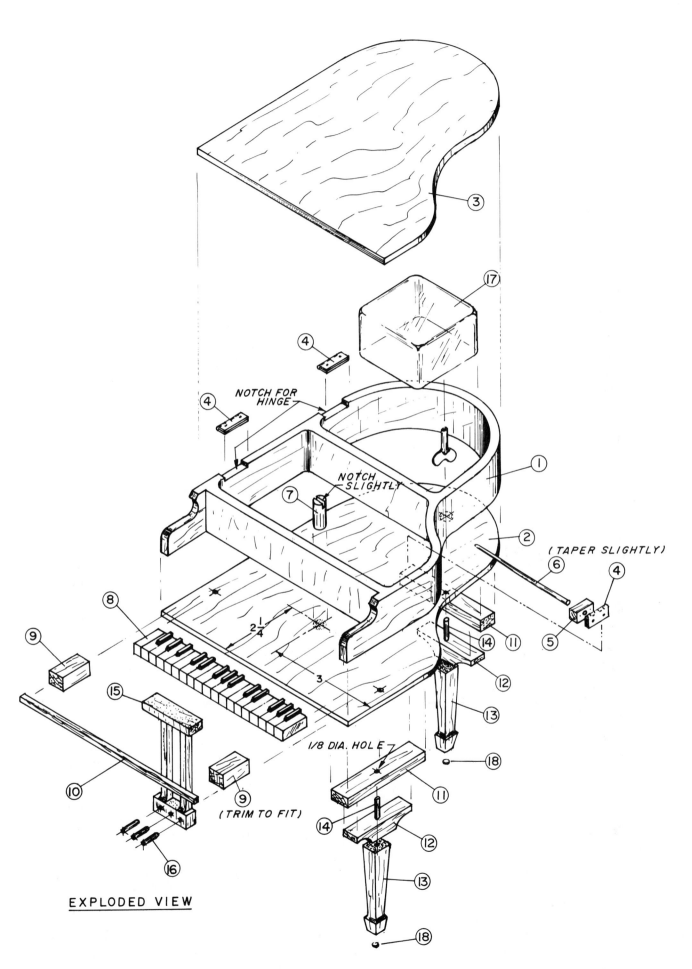

NOTCH FOR HINGE

NOTCH SLIGHTLY

(TAPER SLIGHTLY)

$2\frac{1}{4}$

3

(TRIM TO FIT)

1/8 DIA. HOLE

EXPLODED VIEW

181

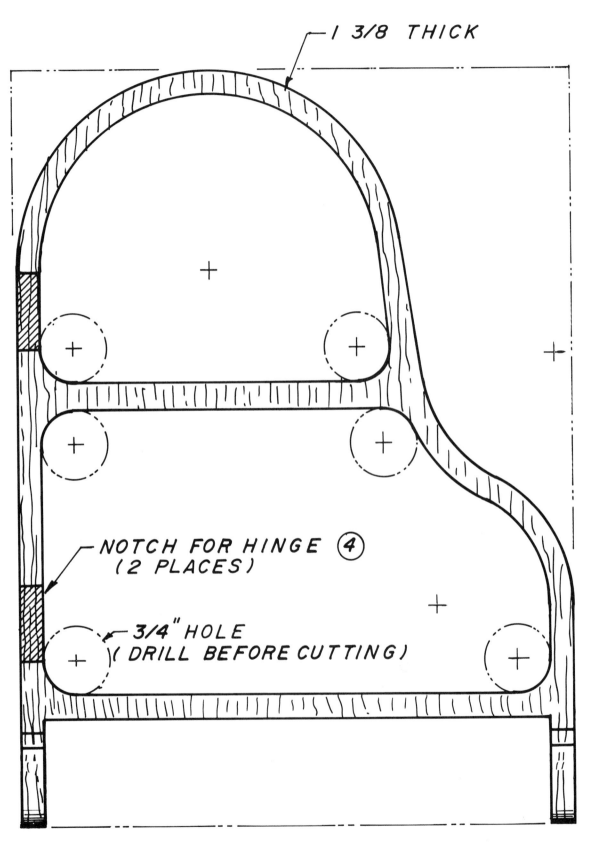

1 3/8 THICK

NOTCH FOR HINGE ④
(2 PLACES)

3/4" HOLE
(DRILL BEFORE CUTTING)

TOP VIEW

BODY ①

FIRST CUT SEE SIDE
VIEW FOR SECOND CUT

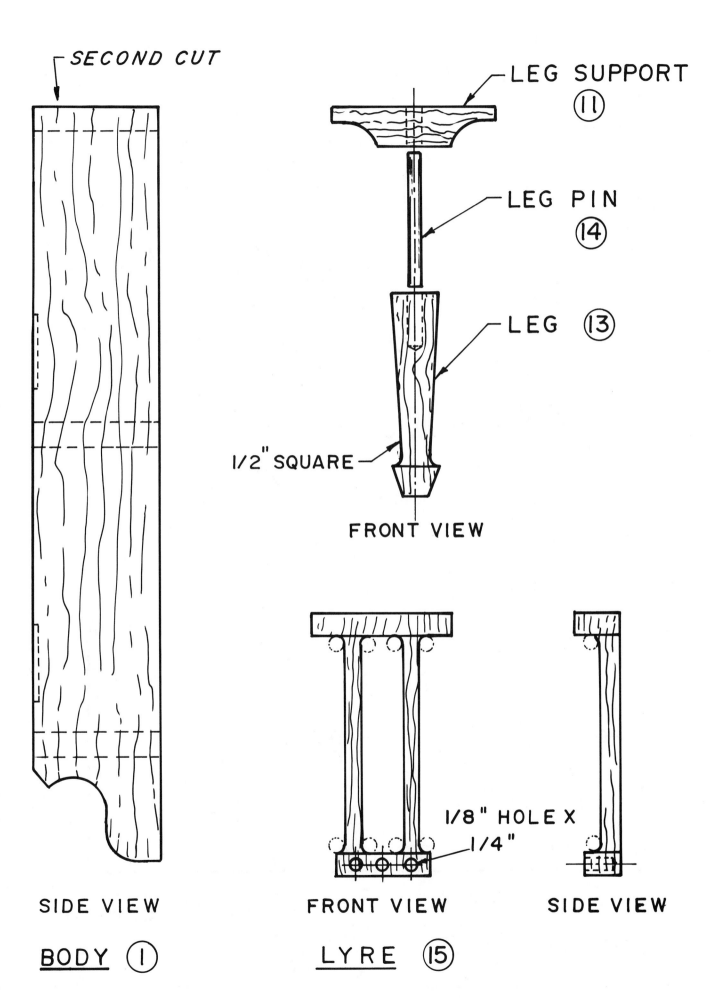

SECOND CUT

LEG SUPPORT ⑪

LEG PIN ⑭

LEG ⑬

1/2" SQUARE

FRONT VIEW

1/8" HOLE X 1/4"

SIDE VIEW

BODY ①

FRONT VIEW　　SIDE VIEW

LYRE ⑮

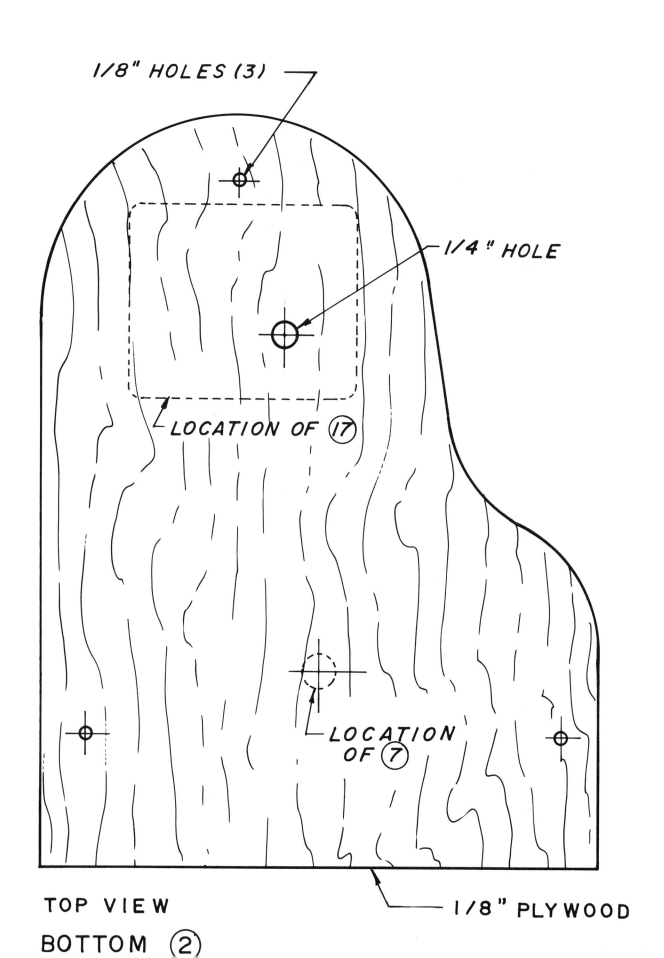

1/8" HOLES (3)

1/4" HOLE

LOCATION OF ⑰

LOCATION OF ⑦

TOP VIEW

BOTTOM ②

1/8" PLYWOOD

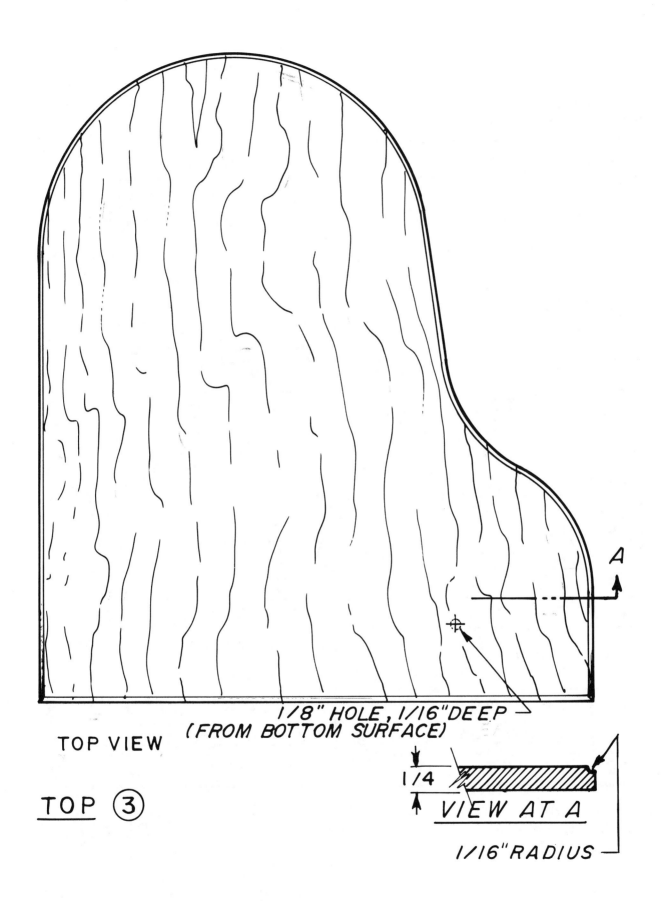

1/8" HOLE, 1/16" DEEP
(FROM BOTTOM SURFACE)

TOP VIEW

TOP ③

A

1/4

VIEW AT A

1/16" RADIUS

185

CAROUSEL

NO	NAME	SIZE	REQ'D.
1	BASE	1/2 X 14 - 14 LONG	1
2	TOP/BOTTOM	1/2 X 15 1/2 - 15 1/2	2
3	BASE TRIM	1/4 X 1 1/8 - 6 3/4 LG	8
4	TOP TRIM	1/4 X 2 - 6 3/4 LG	8
5	SPACER - LARGE	1/2 X 7 1/2 - 7 1/2 LG	2
6	INSIDE WALL	1/4 X 3 3/8 - 6 LG	8
7	TOP TRIM	1/4 X 3/4 - 3 5/8 LG	8
8	BOTTOM TRIM	1/4 X 2 - 3 5/8 LG	8
9	SPACER - SMALL	1/2 X 2 3/4 - 2 3/4	2
10	TOP HOUSING	1/4 X 1 7/16 - 3 LG	8
11	TOP TRIM	1/2 X 3 - 6 7/8 LG	8
12	ROOF	1/2 X 3 - 3 LONG	1
13	BASE FOR BALL	1/4 X 2 DIA.	1
14	TOP BALL	1 1/2 DIA.	1
15	PEG	3/8 DIA. X 2 1/4 LG	1
16	LAZY SUSAN	12" SIZE	1
17	RUBBER FEET	1/2 SIZE	3
18	SUPPORT POLE	1/2 DIA. X 7 LONG	8
19	SUPPORT - HORSE	3/16 DIA. X 6 1/2	8
20	HORSE	1/2 THICK	8

MAKE PARTS NO. 1 AND 3 OUT OF PLYWOOD

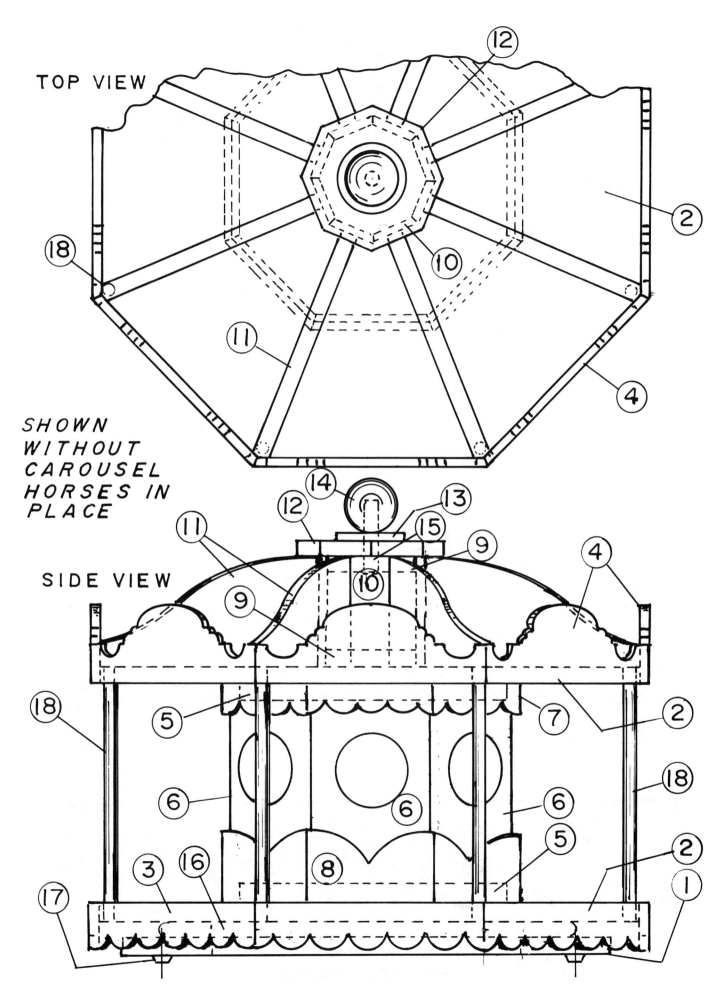

TOP VIEW

SHOWN
WITHOUT
CAROUSEL
HORSES IN
PLACE

SIDE VIEW

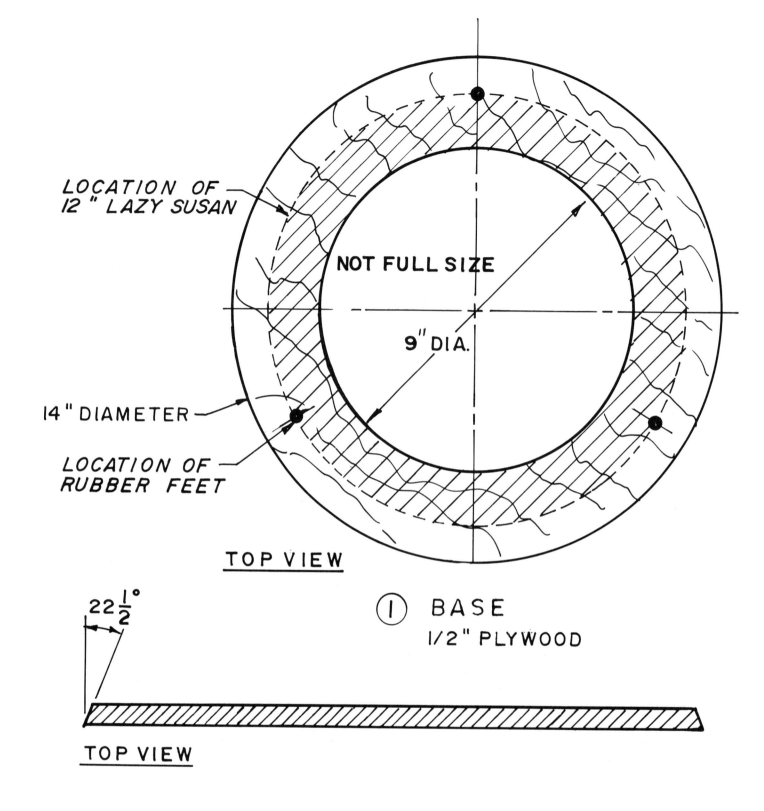

LOCATION OF
12" LAZY SUSAN

NOT FULL SIZE

9" DIA.

14" DIAMETER

LOCATION OF
RUBBER FEET

TOP VIEW

$22\frac{1}{2}°$

TOP VIEW

① BASE
1/2" PLYWOOD

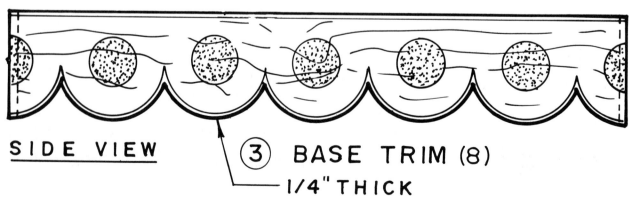

SIDE VIEW

③ BASE TRIM (8)

1/4" THICK

188

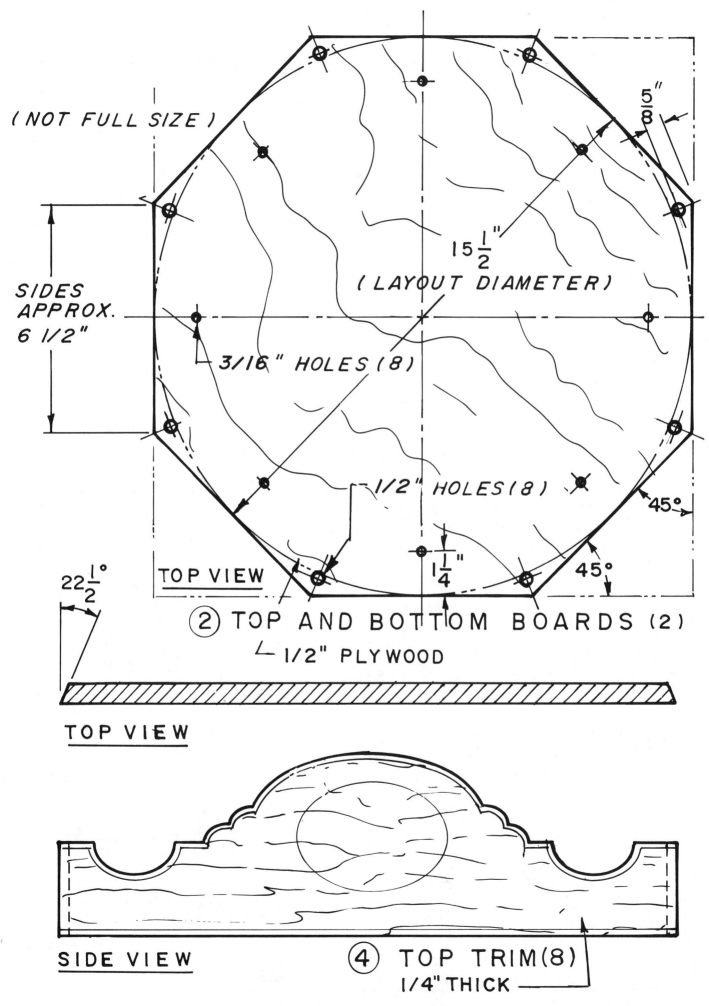

(NOT FULL SIZE)

SIDES
APPROX.
6 1/2"

$15\frac{1}{2}"$
(LAYOUT DIAMETER)

$\frac{5}{8}"$

3/16" HOLES (8)

1/2" HOLES (8)

$1\frac{1}{4}"$

45°

45°

$22\frac{1}{2}°$

TOP VIEW

② TOP AND BOTTOM BOARDS (2)
└ 1/2" PLYWOOD

TOP VIEW

SIDE VIEW   ④ TOP TRIM (8)
1/4" THICK

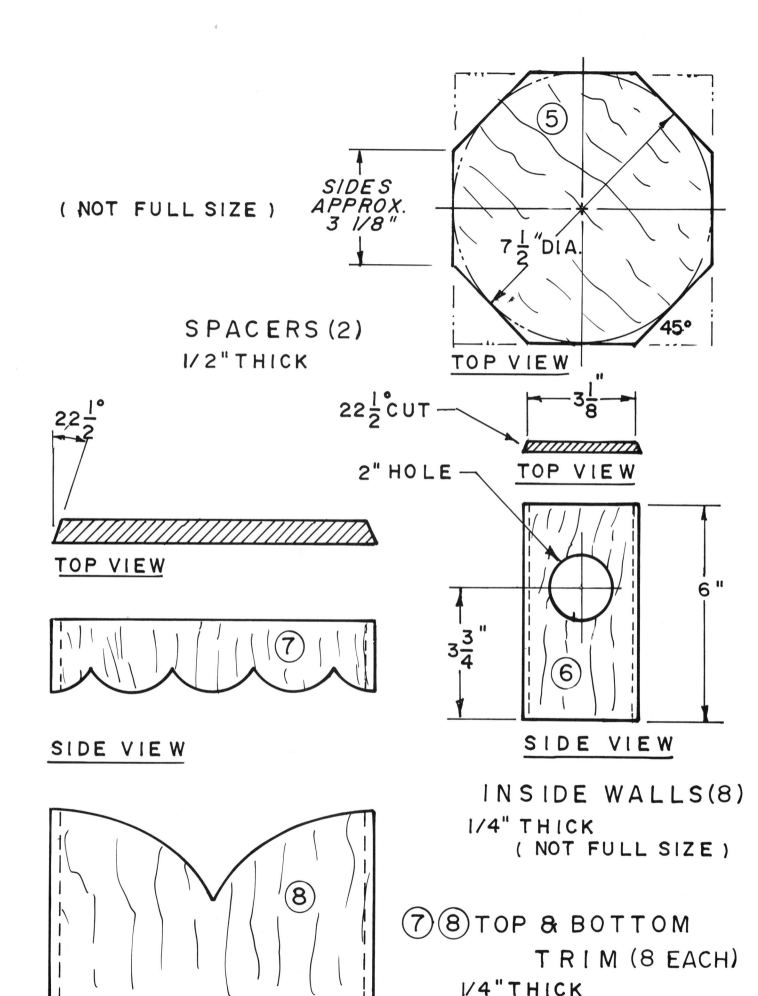

(NOT FULL SIZE)

SPACERS (2)
1/2" THICK

$22\frac{1}{2}°$

TOP VIEW

SIDE VIEW

SIDES APPROX. 3 1/8"

⑤

$7\frac{1}{2}$" DIA.

45°

TOP VIEW

$22\frac{1}{2}°$ CUT

$3\frac{1}{8}$"

TOP VIEW

2" HOLE

$3\frac{3}{4}$"

6"

⑥

SIDE VIEW

INSIDE WALLS (8)
1/4" THICK
(NOT FULL SIZE)

⑦

⑧

⑦ ⑧ **TOP & BOTTOM TRIM (8 EACH)**
1/4" THICK

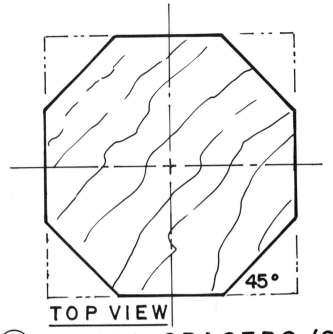

TOP VIEW

⑨ SMALL SPACERS (2)

1/2" THICK

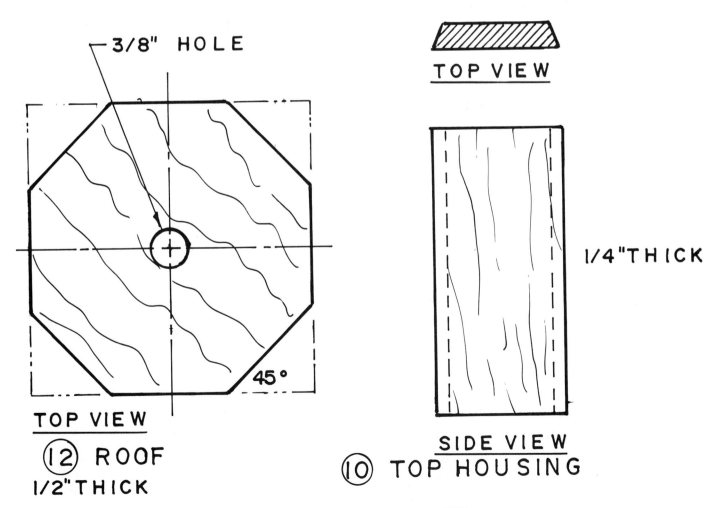

—3/8" HOLE

45°

TOP VIEW

⑫ ROOF

1/2" THICK

TOP VIEW

1/4" THICK

SIDE VIEW

⑩ TOP HOUSING

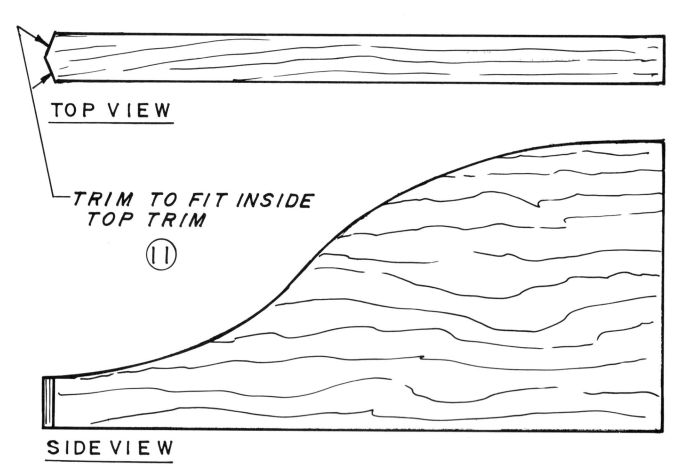

TOP VIEW

TRIM TO FIT INSIDE
TOP TRIM

⑪

SIDE VIEW

TOP TRIM (8)
1/2" THICK

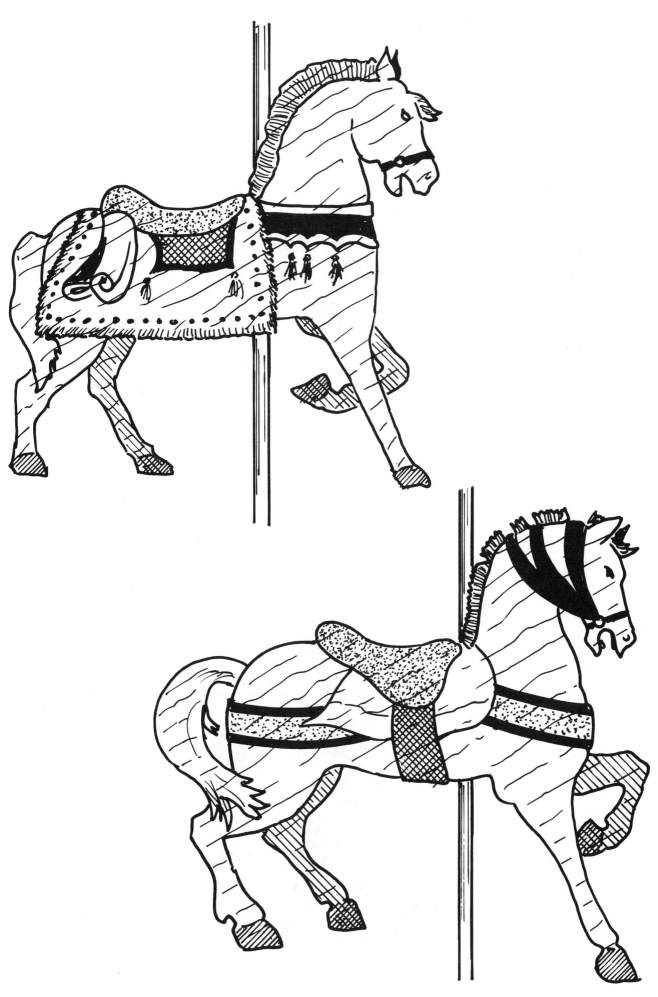

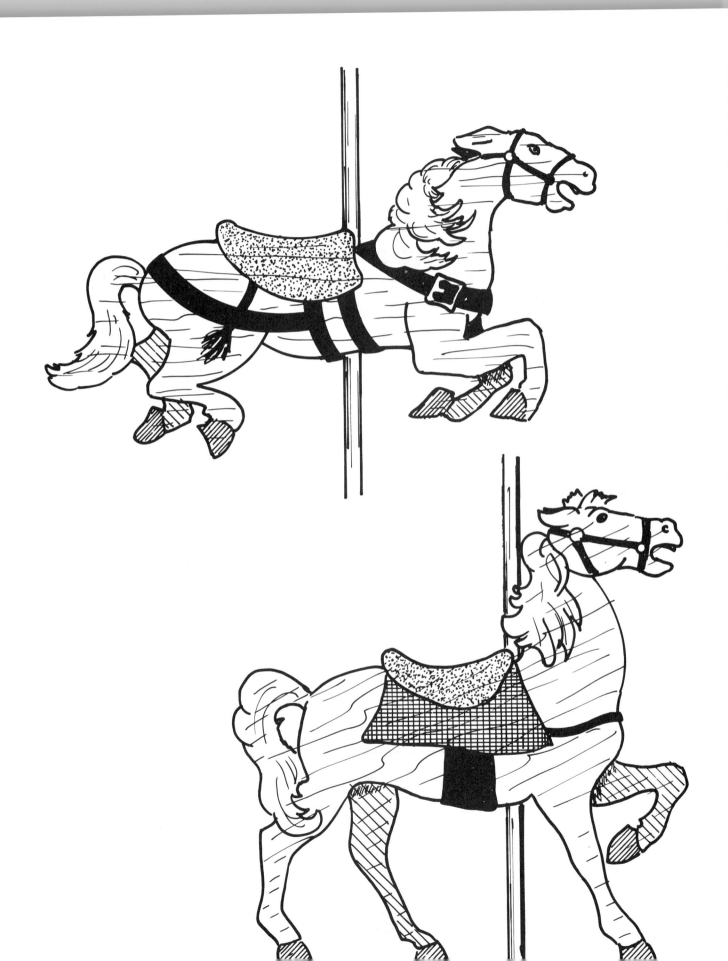

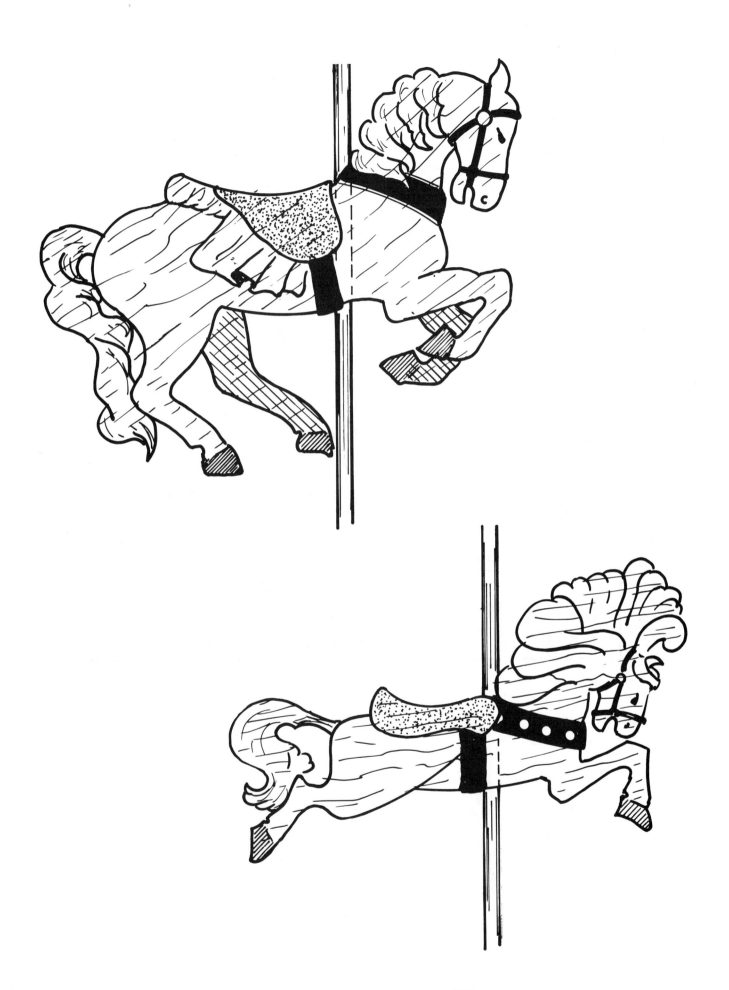

NOAH'S ARK

NO.	NAME	SIZE	REQ'D.
1	BASE	1/2 X 5 1/2 – 10 1/4 LG	1
2	AXLE SUPPORT	1/2 X 1 1/4 – 3 1/2 LG	2
3	WHEEL	1 3/4 DIA.	4
4	AXLE PEG	FOR ABOVE WHEEL	4
5	FRONT	1/2 X 6 – 8 LONG	1
6	BACK	1/2 X 6 – 6 1/2 LONG	1
7	FRONT TRIM	1/4 X 1 3/4 – 7 LG	1
8	RUDDER	1/4 X 1 – 3 LONG	1
9	SIDE	1/4 X 4 – 15 LONG	2
10	FLOOR	1/2 X 5 1/2 – 13 5/8	1
11	CABIN END	1/2 X 4 1/2 – 4 3/4	2
12	CABIN SIDE	1/4 X 2 3/4 – 8 5/8	2
13	ROOF	1/4 X 3 5/8 – 11 1/2	2
14	ROOF SUPPORT	1/4 X 1/2 – 8 1/8 LG	1
15	RAMP	1/4 X 2 – 7 1/2 LG.	1

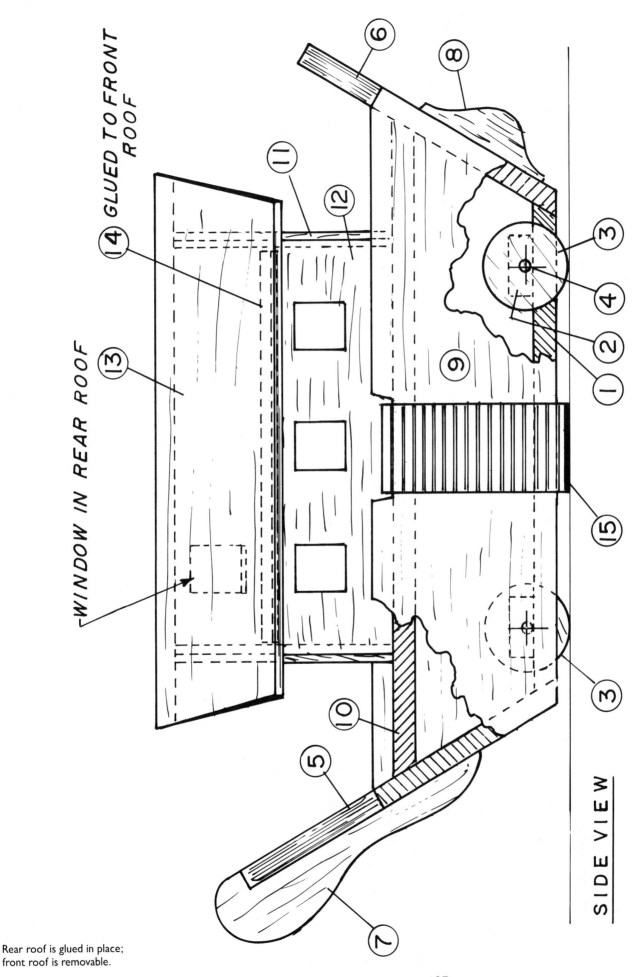

WINDOW IN REAR ROOF

14 GLUED TO FRONT ROOF

Rear roof is glued in place;
front roof is removable.

SIDE VIEW

197

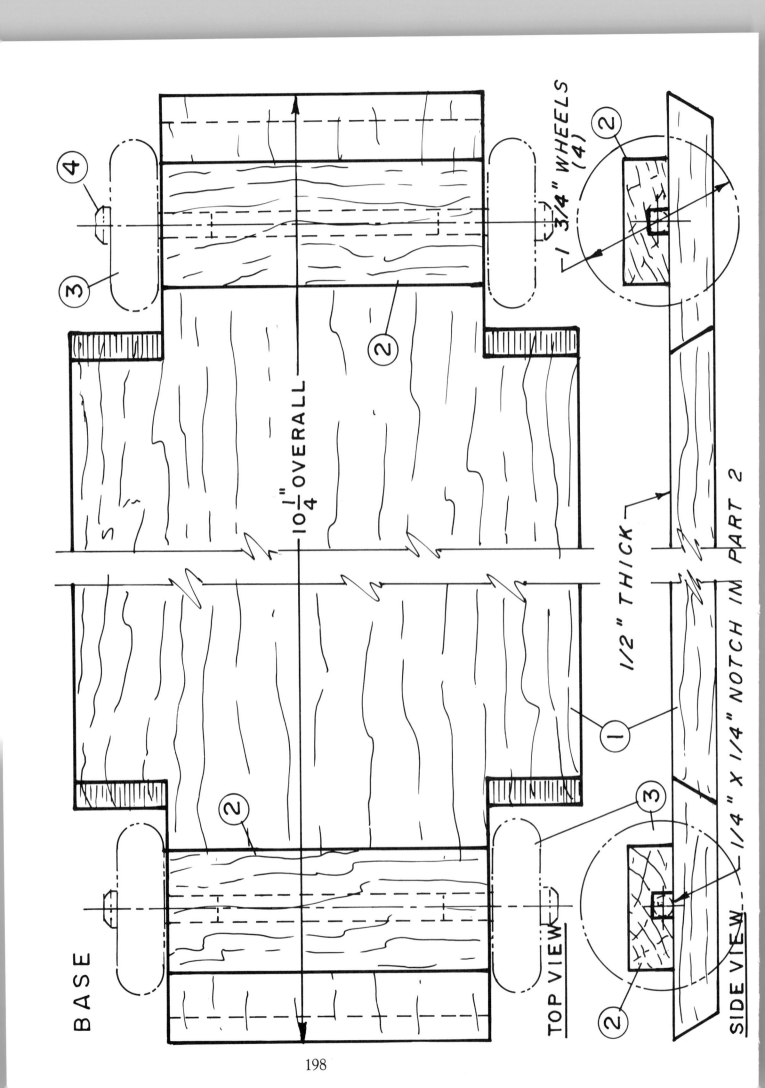

BASE

10 $\frac{1}{4}$" OVERALL

1 $\frac{3}{4}$" WHEELS (4)

1/2" THICK

TOP VIEW

SIDE VIEW — 1/4" X 1/4" NOTCH IN PART 2

FRONT

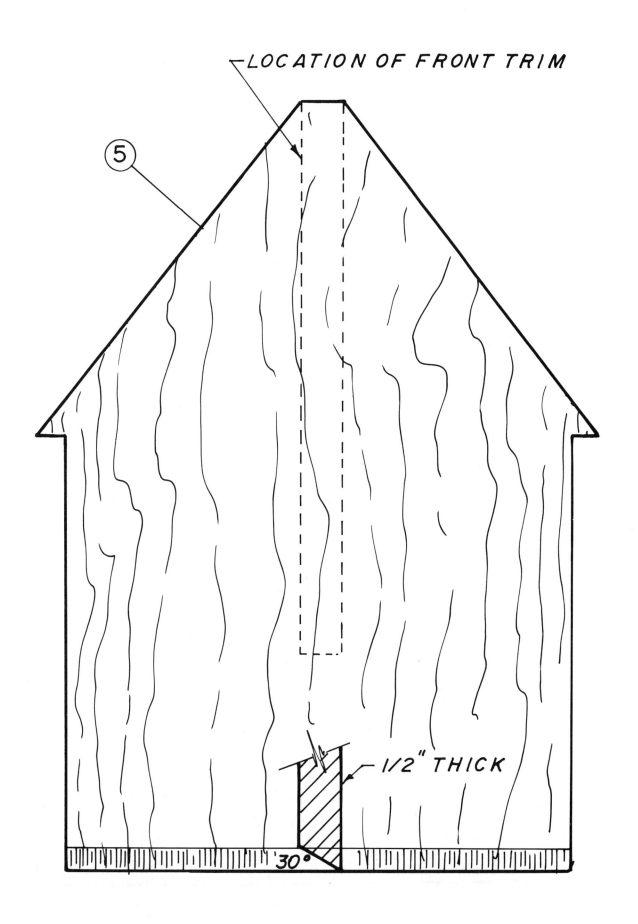

LOCATION OF FRONT TRIM

5

1/2" THICK

30°

199

BACK

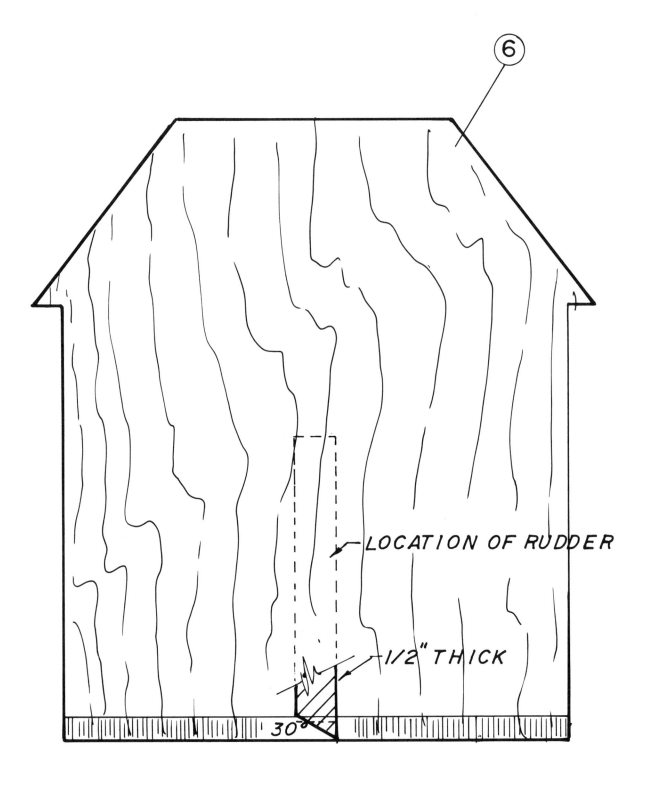

LOCATION OF RUDDER

1/2" THICK

30°

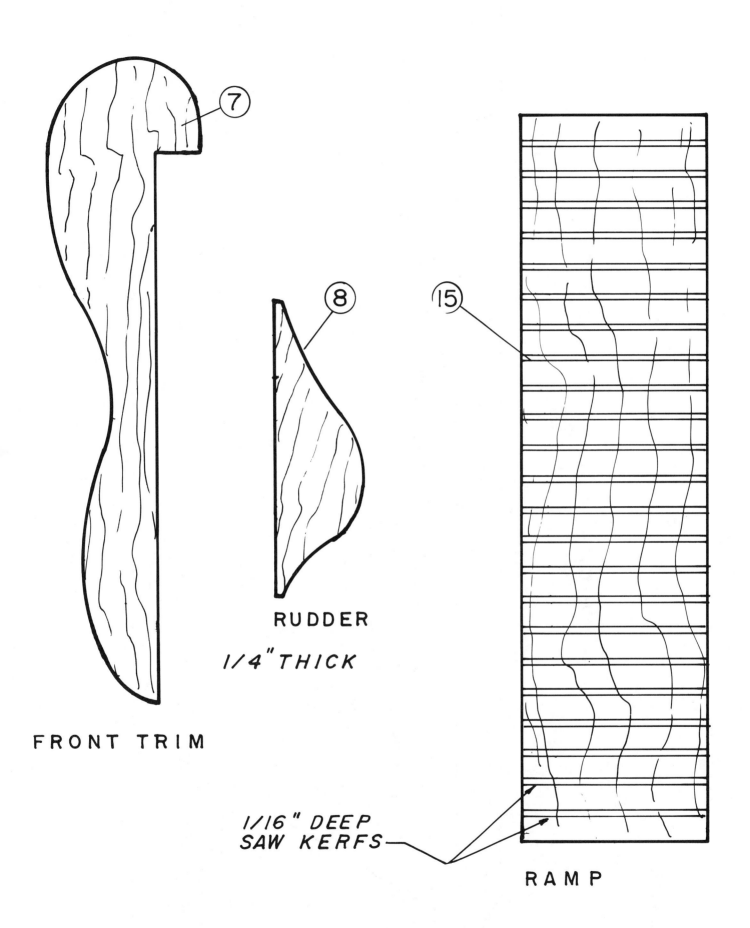

(7)

(8)

RUDDER

1/4" THICK

FRONT TRIM

(15)

1/16" DEEP
SAW KERFS

RAMP

SIDE

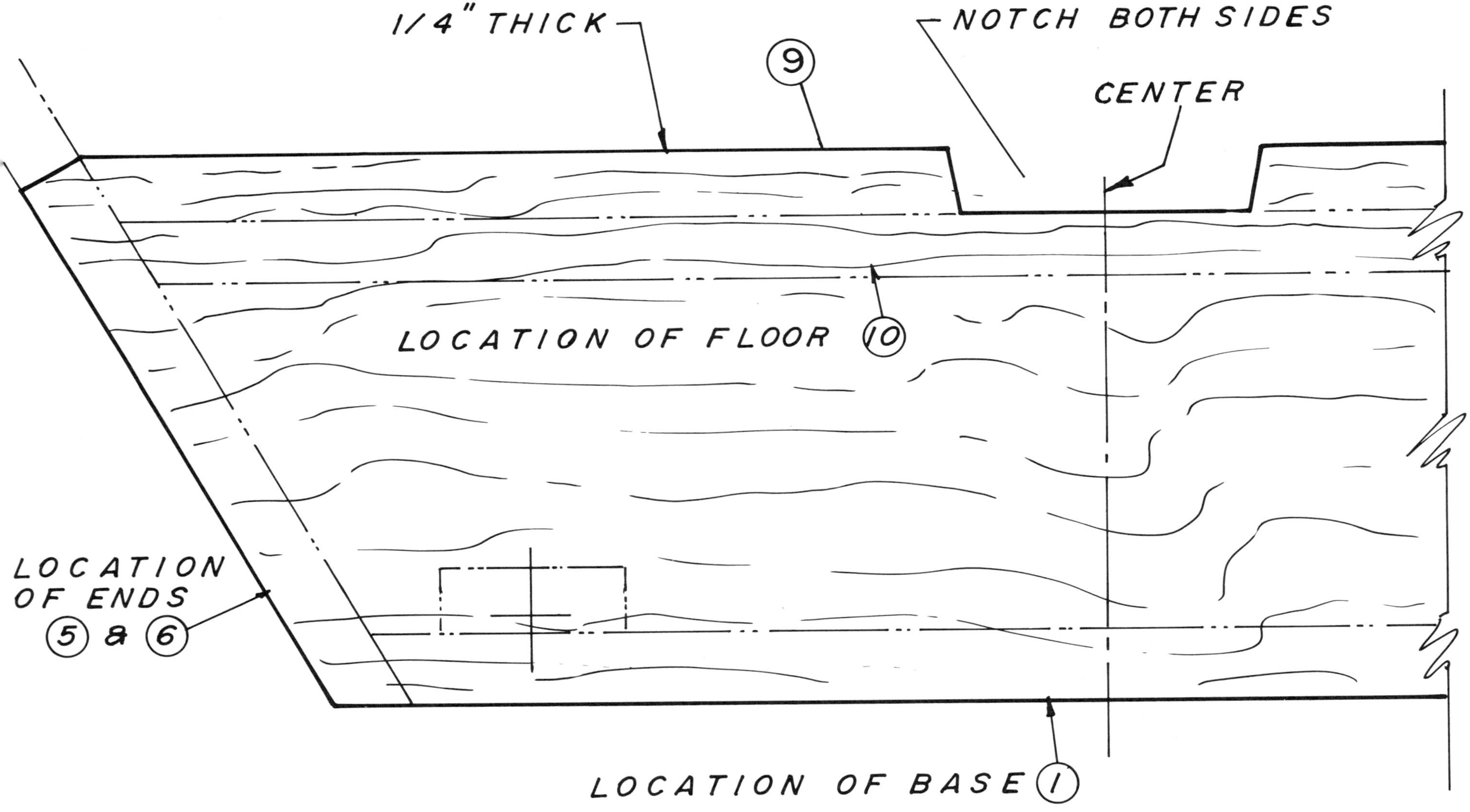

1/4" THICK

NOTCH BOTH SIDES

CENTER

⑨

⑩

LOCATION OF FLOOR

LOCATION OF BASE ①

LOCATION
OF ENDS
⑤ & ⑥

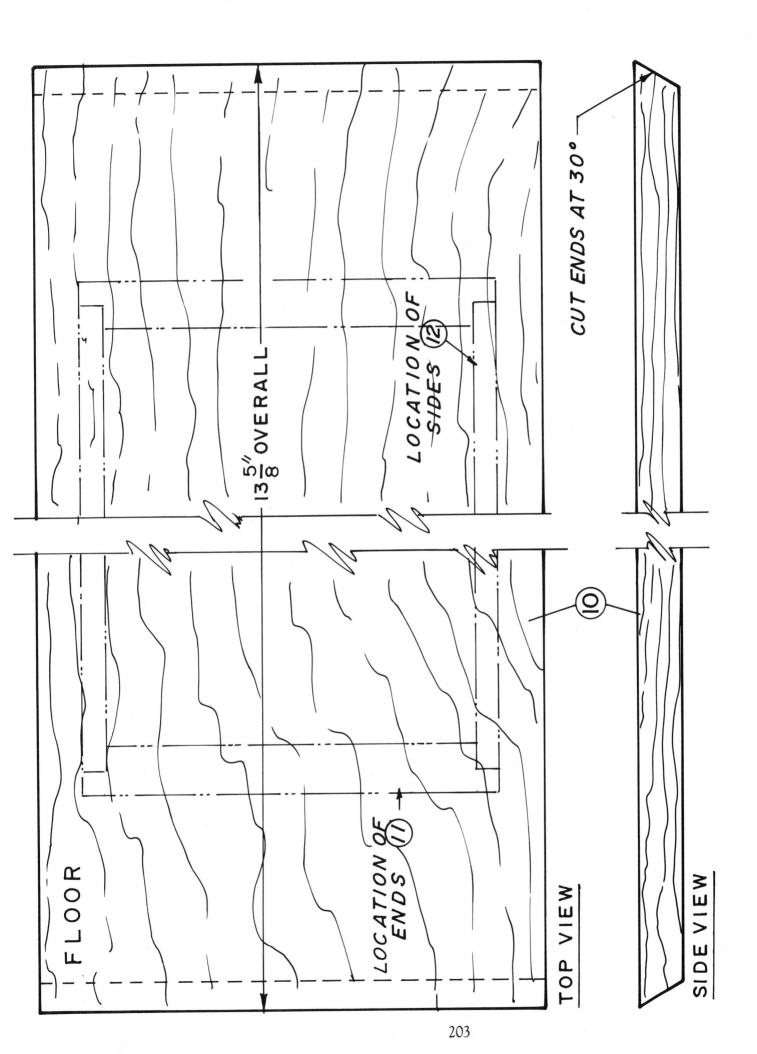

FLOOR

$13\frac{5}{8}"$ OVERALL

LOCATION OF ENDS (11)

LOCATION OF SIDES (12)

(10)

TOP VIEW

CUT ENDS AT 30°

SIDE VIEW

203

CABIN ENDS (2)

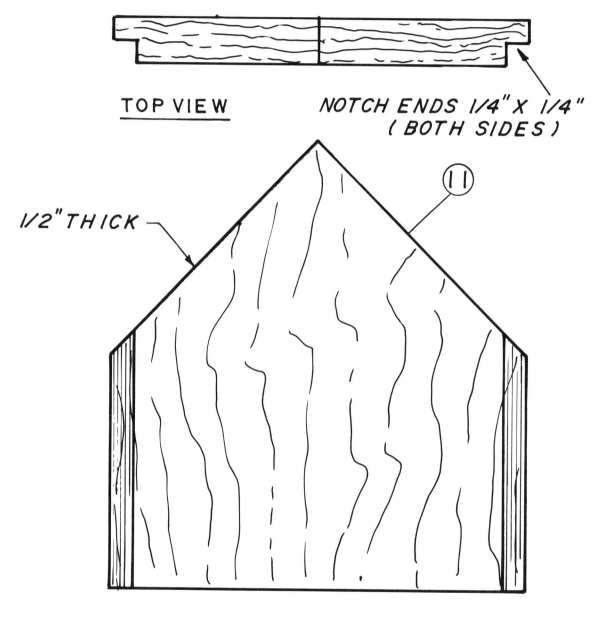

TOP VIEW

NOTCH ENDS 1/4" X 1/4"
(BOTH SIDES)

⑪

1/2" THICK

FRONT VIEW

SIDES (2)

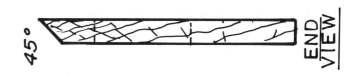

45°

END
VIEW

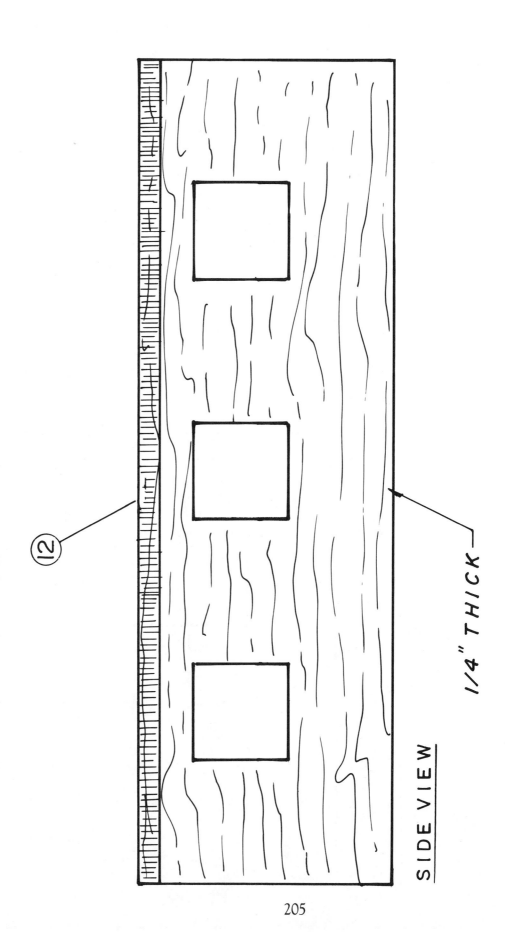

⑫

SIDE VIEW

1/4" THICK

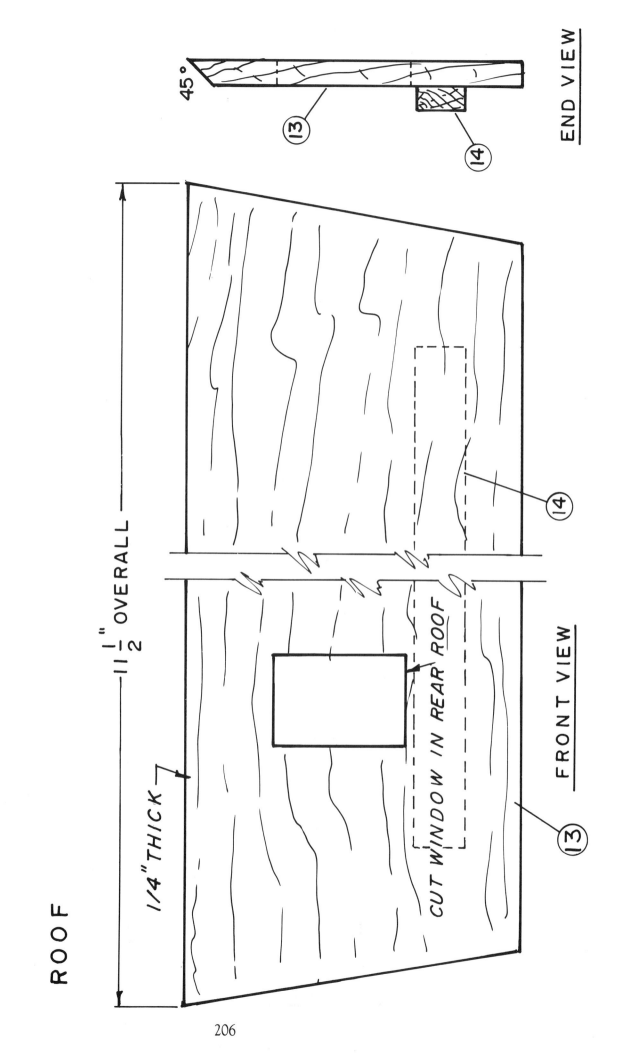

ROOF

END VIEW

45°

⑬

⑭

FRONT VIEW

11½" OVERALL

1/4" THICK

CUT WINDOW IN REAR ROOF

⑭

⑬

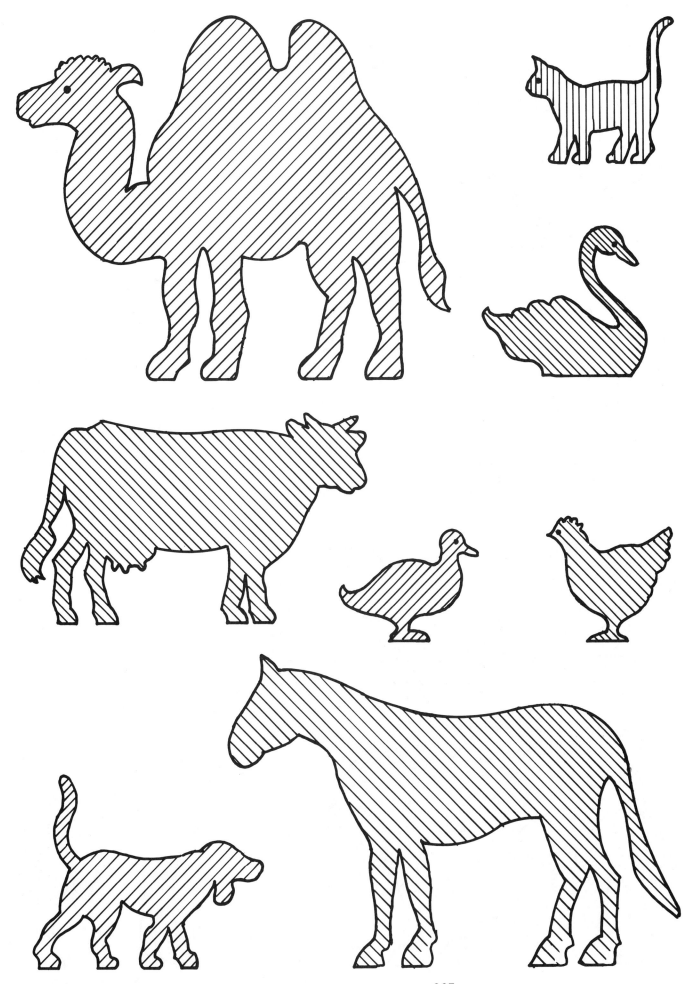

211

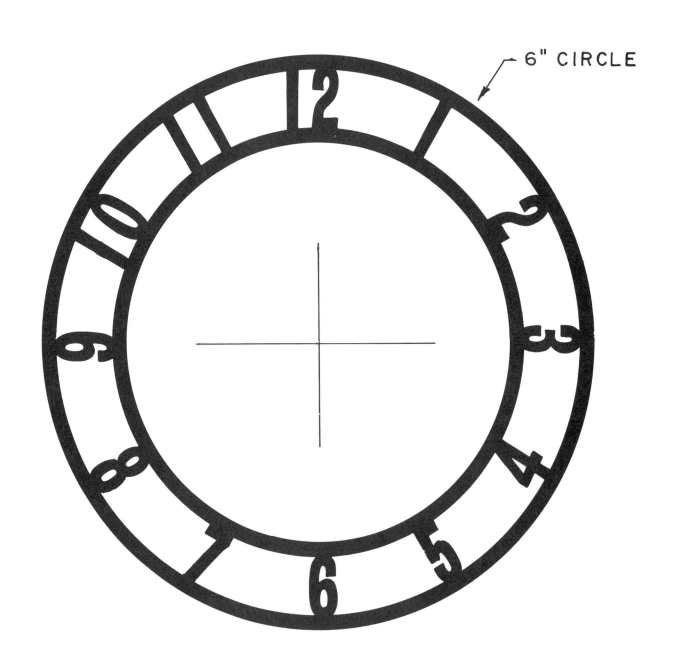

6" CIRCLE

213

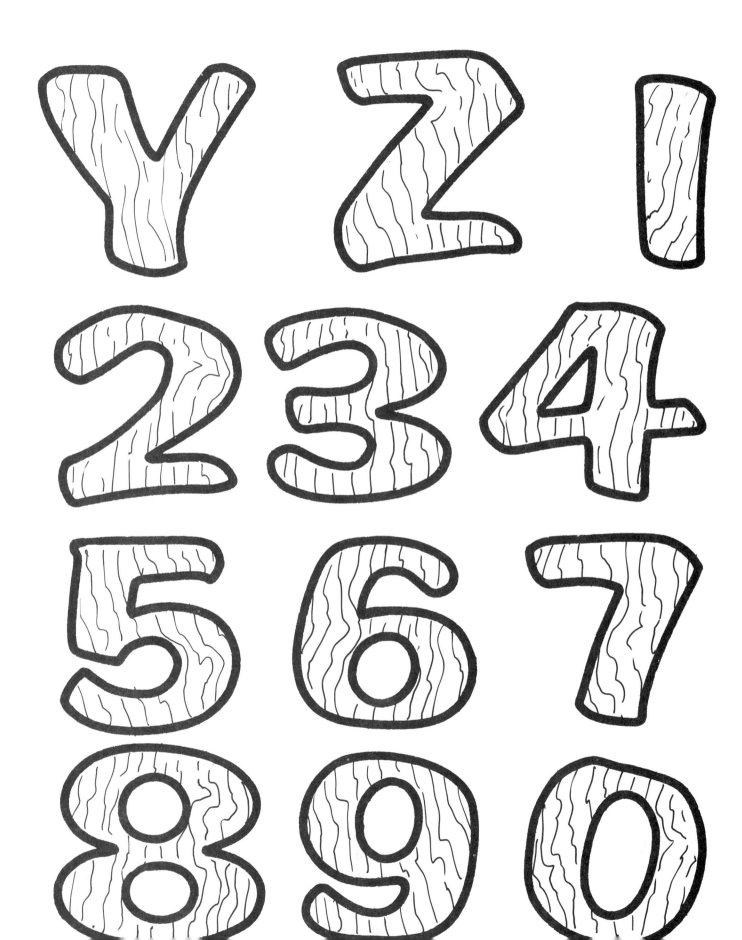

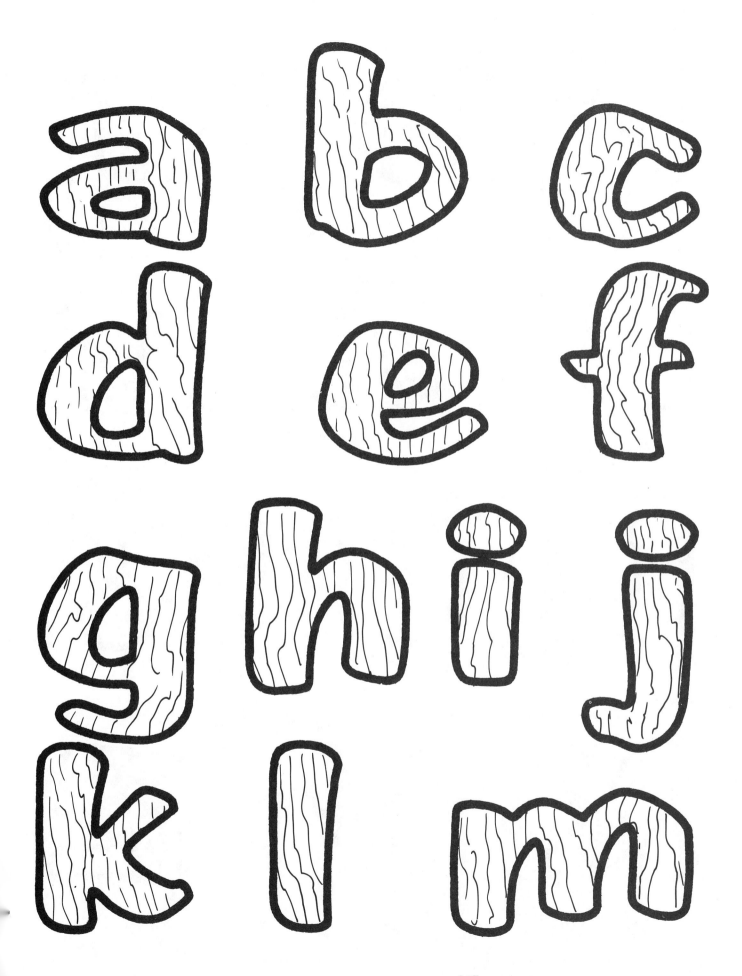

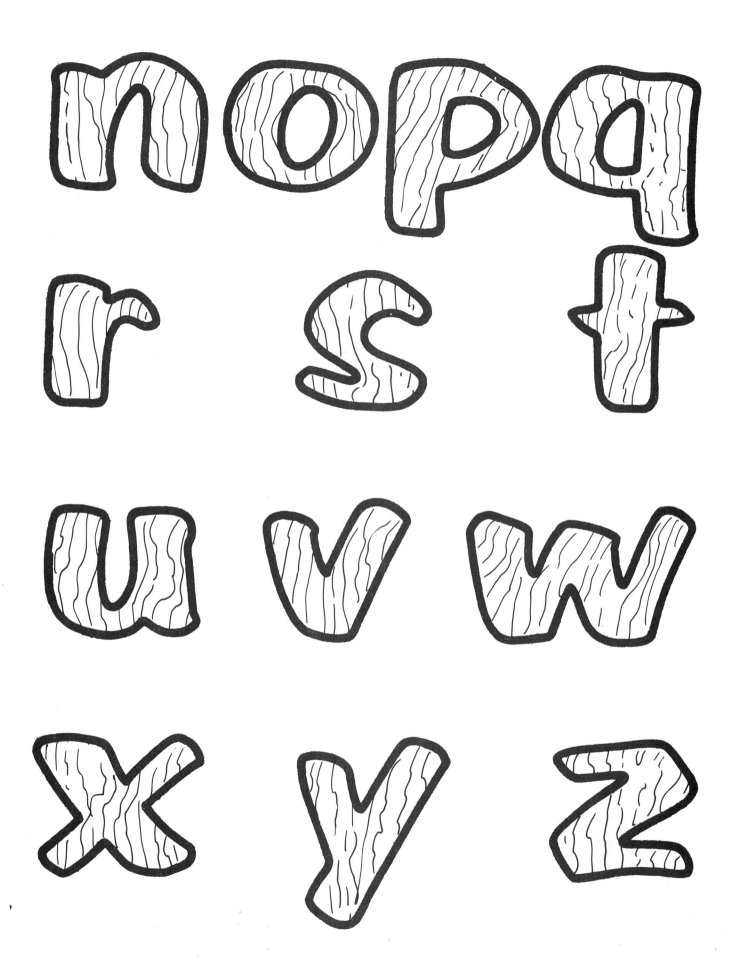

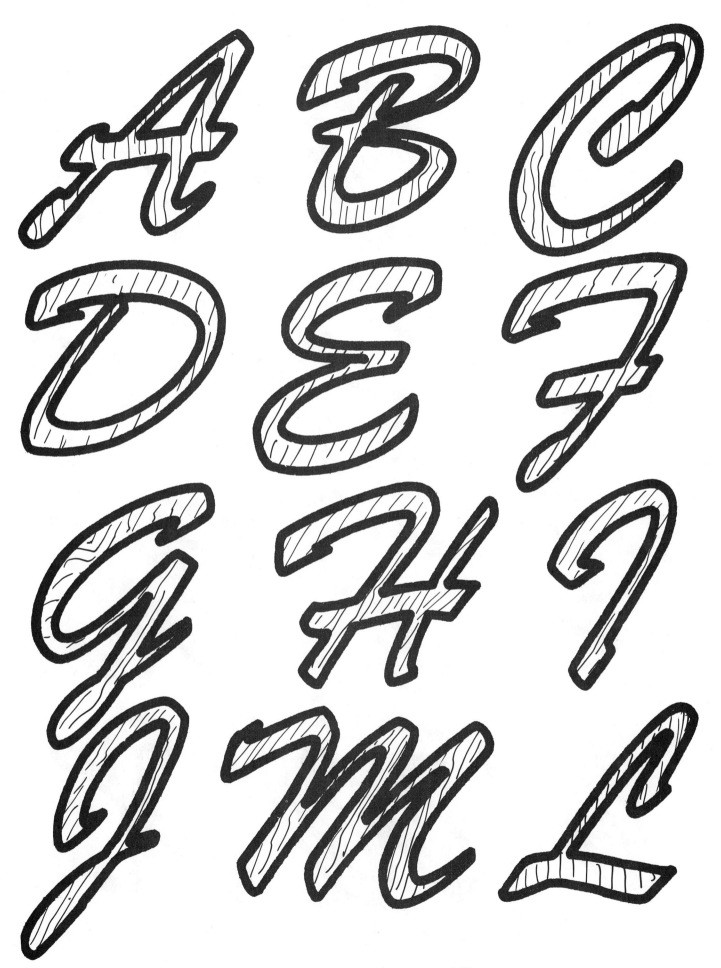

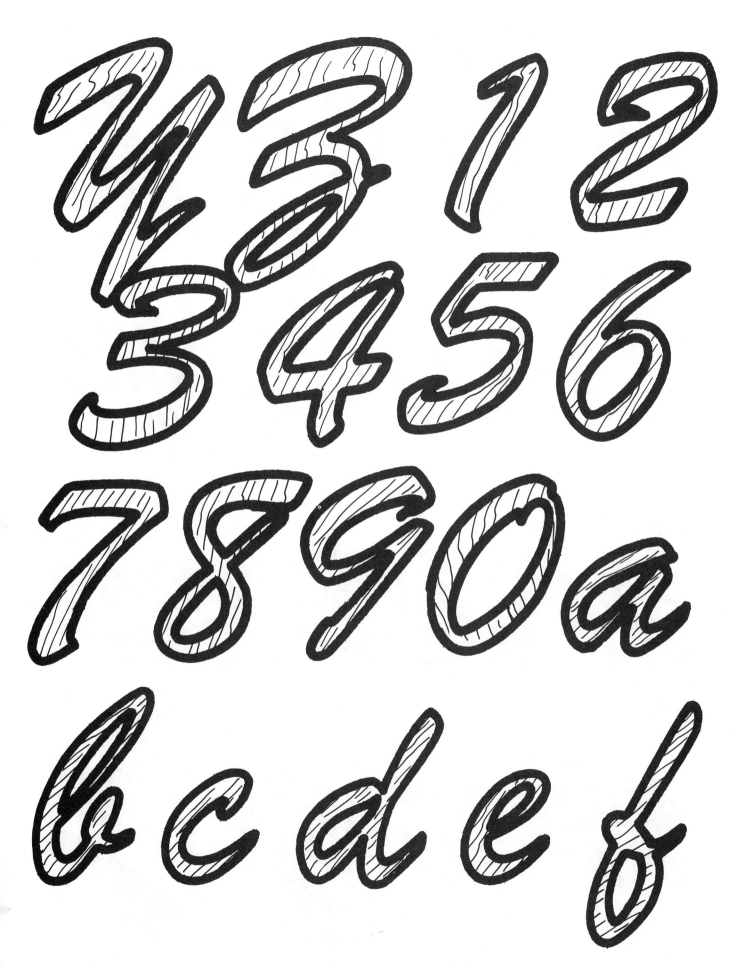

g h i j k

l m n o p

q r s t u v

w x y z

Appendices

SCROLL SAW MANUFACTURERS

American Machine and Tool Co.
P.O. Box 70
4th and Spring Sts.
Royersford, PA 19468

Advanced Machinery Imports Ltd.
  (Hegner saws)
P.O. Box 312
New Castle, DE 19720

Delta International Machinery Corp.
246 Alpha Dr.
Pittsburgh, PA 15238

Dremel
P.O. Box 1468
Racine, WI 53401

Excalibur Machine & Tool Co.
210 Eighth St. South
Lewiston, NY 10492

Glendo Corporation (Heartwood saws)
P.O. Box 1153
Emporia, KS 66801

Jet Equipment and Tools
P.O. Box 1477
Tacoma, WA 98401

R.B. Industries
P.O. Box 369
Harrison, MO 64701

Sears, Roebuck & Co. (Craftsman saws)

Vega Enterprises
R.R. 3, Box 193
Decatur, IL 62526

SUPPLIERS

Cherry Tree Toys
P.O. Box 369
Belmont, OH 43718
614 484-4363

Croffwood Mills (wood only)
R.D. 1, Box 14
Driftwood, PA 15832
800 874-5455

DonJer Products (Suede-Tex only)
Ilene Court, Building 8
Belle Mead, NJ 08502
800 336-6537

Klockit (clock movements)
P.O. Box 636
Lake Geneva, WI 53147
800 556-2548

Leichtung Workshops
4944 Commerce Pkwy.
Cleveland, OH 44128
800 321-6840

Meisel Hardware Specialties
P.O. Box 70
Mound, MN 55364
800 441-9870

Rainbow Woods
20 Andrews St.
Newnan, GA 30263
800 423-2762

RJS Custom Woodworking
P.O. Box 12354
Kansas City, KS 66112

Timbers Woodworking
Timbers Building
Selma, OR 97538
800 762-5385

Wheelwright (cast pewter wheels only)
3500 63rd St.
Saugatuck, MI 49453
616 857-1724

Woodentoy
P.O. Box 40344
Grand Junction, CO 81504

BLADES

Blades are available from all the saw
manufacturers and also from the following
suppliers:

American Intertool Inc.
1255 Tonne
Elk Grove Village, IL 60007
708 640-7766

Olson Saw Company
16 Stony Hill
Bethel, CT 06801
203 792-8622